REFUGEE ENTERPRISE
It can be done

Chris Rolfe, Clare Rolfe and Malcolm Harper

INTERMEDIATE TECHNOLOGY PUBLICATIONS 1987

For all those who came for the emergency and stayed into development...

And for those who came to develop and strayed into relief......

And for those who help them, in both endeavours.

AND for the patience and abilities of the refugees - who really do it!

ACKNOWLEDGEMENTS

We would like to thank the very many individuals and agencies that contributed to this study. Particular thanks go to the United Nations High Commission for Refugees in Pakistan and Geneva and to the seven organizations for their case studies:

>   Action International Contre la Faim
>   ACORD (EuroAction ACORD)
>   Austrian Relief Committee
>   American Friends Service Committee/Quaker Peace and Service
>   Christian Outreach
>   Gesellschaft fur Technische Zusammanarbeit (GTZ)
>   World Bank (Pakistan)

The study itself was funded by a research grant from the Overseas Development Administration of the British Government.

The photographs on p.46 are printed with kind permission from:

>   Quaker Peace and Service - "Hassan the Stone-cutter"
>   Austrian Relief Committee - "Abdida the Tailor"
>   Partnership for Productivity - "Mohammed the Dress-maker"
>   (PfP photographer Pirkko Tanttu)

Intermediate Technology Publications Ltd
9 King Street, London, WC2E 8HW, UK

The authors and the publishers wish to thank the Overseas Development Administration of the British Government for its financial support of the research for this book, and its printing, though it should be stressed that the views expressed are those of the authors and do not necessarily represent the views of the ODA.

© Intermediate Technology Publications 1987
ISBN 0 946688 59 1

Printed in Great Britain by Russell Press Ltd., Gamble Street, Nottingham NG7 4ET.

HOW TO USE THIS BOOK

The authors' main intention in this book is to encourage interest in Refugee Enterprise. The book is also designed for field workers involved in starting or running refugee income-generating (IG) programmes. It can therefore be used in two ways:

1) As a book to read through from beginning to end. It is in five parts:
- Introduction - the background of the book and the people involved.
- Framework for Thinking - setting up a theory for analysing types of income-generating project.
- Case studies - five case studies of succesful programmes and five case studies of refugee businesses.
- "A to Z" - practical points on aspects of "IG".
- Appendices - the questionnnaire survey results used to support points in the manual and other information, such as contacts and a booklist.

2) As a reference book, an "A to Z", of information on IG topics. In this case, the following two paragraphs will summarize the introduction, theory and appendices, so the reader may immediately turn to the "A to Z":

This book is concerned with income-generating projects for refugees from poor countries and now in poor host countries, such as Ethiopian refugees in Somalia or Afghan refugees in Pakistan. Many of these refugees cannot return home. They are neither allowed to become local citizens, nor can they expect a third country to take them. As aid to the refugees is slowly withdrawn, they need to be more self-reliant, but there are many constraints. Taking a wide definition of income-generating activities, outside agencies can help these refugees. Help can come from relief agencies starting to look beyond the relief phase, or from development agencies adjusting their regular activities to the more restricted situation of refugees.

The analysis is based on a questionnaire survey of 153 IG programmes, of which 23 were in detail, as well as the authors' personal experience. There seem to be eight types of programme, all gradually changing from relief type assistance to development style self-sufficiency, and all operating within the limits of the host country:

1. Relief Substitution - Refugees making relief items for themselves.
2. Development Investment - Refugees involved with infrastructural or environmental improvements to their new location.
3. Income-adding Starters - Very simple, cheap assistance, such as chickens or gardens, which add or save income, but are not full businesses.
4. Basic Skill Utilization - Using refugees' skills in farming or handicrafts.
5. Vocational Training and Production Schemes - Improving refugees' skills.
6. Business Starter Schemes - Helping start businesses, e.g. providing some tools.
7. Business Assistance - Range of assistance for new and existing businesses.
8. Employment Bureaux - Helping place refugees in refugee or local businesses.

TABLE OF CONTENTS

	Page number
INTRODUCTION	4
The Study behind the Book	5
Objectives and Limitations	6
A FRAMEWORK FOR THINKING	
The Position of Refugees for Development	7
Types and Timing of Income-generating Projects	10
The Position of Refugees after the Relief Phase	15
CASE STUDIES (Five agency programmes and five refugee businesses)	
PAKISTAN	
Assistance to skilled refugees-Action International Contre La Faim	17
Expanding out of relief - Austrian Relief Committee	20
SOMALIA	
After relief what? - The British and American Quakers	24
SUDAN	
The Business End - ACORD in Port Sudan	34
The Relief End - Christian Outreach in East Sudan	39
Agency Comparisons - of these five agencies and their work	42
Three Refugee Businesses and Two "Typical" Refugee Businesses	45
FACTORS FOR CONSIDERATION - BEFORE STARTING	
A For All Agencies	48
B For Relief Agencies Thinking about Development	54
C For Development Agencies Thinking about Refugees	56
D Programme Objectives	58
E Planning Projects	61
F Time-scales	68
CHOOSING AND RUNNING AN INCOME-GENERATING PROJECT	
G Choosing the Type of Project	69
H Relief Substitution - Projects by refugees for refugees	72
I Development Investment - Infrastructure/Environment Projects	74
J Income-adding Starters - Starting Self-help	77
K Basic Skill Utilisation - Agriculture and Village Crafts	79
L Vocational Training and Production Schemes	81
M Business Starter Schemes - For Refugee Entrepreneurs	83
N Business Assistance Projects - For New and Existing Businesses	85
O Employment Bureaux	87
FURTHER DETAILS	
P Possible Projects and Businesses - A List	88
Q Questions on the Selection of Participants	90
R The Refugees' Viewpoint	96
S Women's Projects	97
T First Steps in Marketing - A Checklist	99
U Loans and Guarantees	101
V Non-Financial Assistance	111
W What about the Hosts?	113
X Ending the Project	114
Y Evaluation	116
Z Concluding Comments	125

APPENDICES

Methodology	127
Contact List	128
Bibliography and References	134
Covering Letter to Questionnaire	136
Summary of Questionnaire Replies -	
Questionnaire A Results - Programme Statistics	138
Questionnaire B Results - Qualitative factors for success	142
Questionnaire C Results - Refugee Businesses	148

PHOTOGRAPHS

Three Refugee Businesses	46

LIST OF FIGURES

Figure 1 - Refugee Solutions up to the mid 1970s	8
Figure 2 - Refugee Solutions from the mid 1970s	8
Figure 3 - Income-generating projects: relief to development	13

LIST OF TABLES

Case-study Comparisons (Tables 1-4)

Table 1 - Income-generating Types, Training and Skills	42
Table 2 - Time-scales and Staffing	43
Table 3 - Numbers and Costs	43
Table 4 - Issues of Coverage and Participation	44
Table 5 - IG Project Types and Costs	50
Table 6 - Comparing Income-adding Starters to Business Starters to Business Assistance Projects	83
Table 7 - Business Problems and Assistance - as seen by refugees	96
Table 8 - How refugees Assist their own Businesses	101

EXAMPLE FORMS

Quaker Business Analysis Form	105
Quaker Loan Agreement Form	106
ACROSS Loan Contract	107

INTRODUCTION

Throughout the world millions of refugees remain in poor host countries. "Durable" (long-term) solutions of repatriation (return), resettlement into a third country or integration in the host country are as yet unclear, although the relief phase is over. The question is WHAT NOW ?

For the refugee, who may be a peasant or a university graduate and who may be living in a closed camp or amongst the local people, the answer is given as "income-generation".

Yet the topic "income-generation" with refugees can be like trying to build on shifting sand. There are the relief agencies tentatively doing development, and there are development agencies who complain at refugees' dependency. There are the political factors of land, time-scale and aid - all shifting. And, more importantly, there are the refugees themselves who are at one moment expected to be helpless, and at the next independent.

Looking back at the economic history of many countries it may be seen that although the arrival of refugees always brought complications, it also brought a group of people who had no option but to be innovative. New enterprises and new ideas enriched the host countries. Refugees' skills and strengths did not take away from the national effort - they added to it.

It is important to stress at the beginning that income-generation and self-employment projects can never be a panacea for all the problems of refugees. Entrepreneurs are a small proportion of any population, though this proportion can vary. Indeed, for refugees, the lack of employment opportunities may increase the proportion wishing to try self-employment. And for refugees in and from poorer countries, the modest level of capital and skills required may make it relatively easier to become self-employed. Both these factors may increase their interest in self-employment, but there is still a danger that income-generation may be seen as an answer for all. It is not, and the following groups of refugees fall outside the scope of this study:

- Refugees who have already advanced beyond the need for "aid";
  may we wish them continued success.
- Refugees for whom employment by someone else is a better option;
  it may be they have the skills, but lack the determination and motivation
  to make a success of a business on their own.
- Refugees whose situation does not enable them to participate in such income-
  generating projects. There is no group that can be excluded automatically,
  but individual refugees may have the problems of being elderly, sick, single
  parents or handicapped, and since these individuals can form relatively large
  proportions of refugee numbers, they must be included in the planning of projects.
  Many carefully targetted projects can and do help these groups of people.

However, income-generation and self-employment projects do play an important part in helping refugees to move away from the dependency which comes from receiving aid during the emergency or relief phases. Our intention in this book is to examine some projects which try to help those refugees who want to help themselves. In that situation, the refugees see these projects as an opportunity and most such projects have waiting lists of some description.

We have identified at least 153 projects around the world, though there may be two or three times this number. There are many project proposals and reports, but few overviews or handbooks on this topic, perhaps because the "durable" solutions were generally possible until the mid-late 1970s, except for the Palestinians.

We must now have "flexible" solutions, which are developmental in approach, but accept constraints as to the uncertainties of time of stay, acceptability to their hosts and the availability of resources. In the research, which forms the backbone of this book, we cannot identify a model or models for IG which will work in all situations, because there are so many and varying constraints. Instead, we give an outline of the many factors, within a framework of moving gradually away from relief style aid. A successful project in one part of the world would be a failure in each new place as the conditions are different. Better to choose and mix the different possibilities, appropriate to the people and the place.

It is not easy. We can only offer some possible hints and some success stories and the encouragement that "It Can Be Done".

THE STUDY BEHIND THE BOOK
This book came to be written through a chance meeting between Malcolm Harper, whose experience is in enterprise development for developing countries and Chris and Clare Rolfe, two community workers from England wrestling with "income-generation" in a Somali Refugee Camp. There followed a six month study, from July to December 1986, by the Cranfield School of Management's Enterprise Development Centre, funded by the British Goverment's Overseas Development Administration (ODA).

We sent letters to 103 international aid agencies asking for further contact addresses in the refugee asylum countries for a postal survey of refugee income-generating projects. Using these replies, we sent 79 full questionnaires of which 23 were returned.

The full questionnaire included a five page Questionnaire A. on the background and statistics of the project or programme; a six page Questionnaire B. on the qualitative factors for the success of refugee IG projects; and twenty copies of the two page Questionnaire C. for individual refugee businesses. One hundred and twenty four of the refugee business questionnaires were returned from five countries.

During this process we obtained some information on 153 IG programmes in 43 countries. We also visited agency head offices and researchers in Europe for more information and added seven more replies to Questionnaire B. One short visit to Pakistan was also included to check the preliminary results and to compare the authors' experiences of Somalia and Sudan against another setting. All the information was analyzed on a microcomputer and the results and methodology are in the appendices. The analysis of this study and the other information collected form the backbone of this book.

The authors had some previous experiences of refugee income-generating projects: Malcolm Harper was a consultant to the Euro Action Acord Port Sudan Project and to a project in North-West Somalia for Partnership for Productivity (PfP). Chris and Clare Rolfe worked for three years on a range of income-generating projects in one camp in North-West Somalia, and then as trainers to the PfP business advisors in that project. These experiences are used in the case studies and background, but not in the questionnaire analysis, to avoid a biased result.

Because of the short time-scale we have limited the scope of the study, to the objectives set out on the next page, but we hope others will be able to extend from this.

OBJECTIVES AND LIMITATIONS OF THIS STUDY

Objectives
1. Little is known, and still less published, about refugee entrepreneurs and their businesses or income-generating activities and the ways they can be assisted. The purpose of this research is to identify as many agencies as possible running IG programmes, to find out what they are doing, their success, and to evolve guidelines to assist others trying to do the same.

2. We have tried to concentrate on the decisions which have to be made in programme design, types of enterprise and financial assistance.

Limitations of Study
1. Income-generation or "IG" is really a catch all term for anything that has not its own "named" sector - such as Health, Education, Water, Agriculture or others. It often includes employment, training, income-adding schemes, self-employment, business development, even self-help and community development. Our broad definition retains most of this - "Any activity which will at some time bring in income." Later we try and separate out the different types.

2. We included only refugees who came from and are now in the economically poorer countries. This excludes many refugee income-generation projects in the richer countries, though we included these in our own background reading and some cross-fertilisation seems useful.

3. We excluded "settlements", where refugees have been given land and are expected to remain and to form a permanent part of the local economy. There is already some research and theoretical framework in this field, which formed a useful background to our work.

4. We excluded "closed" camps, where IG is not welcome, although it may be happening. We also excluded illegal activities such as smuggling, prostitution or drugs, though these may be substantial in generating income. We did include, where we found it, the informal or "black" economy, though it is not significant in this study.

5. It is clear the majority of refugees' IG activities are self-started and owe nothing to external assistance. However, lack of time meant the study is mainly concerned with agencies' IG projects. Only 24 out of 124 refugee business people questioned had started on their own with no assistance. There seemed to be no significant differences between them and those who had been assisted - however further studies must include work on this.

6. We did not systematically cross-check or verify the information sent us, although in the few cases where this was possible no discrepancies appeared.

7. We concentrated on projects which were in operation in 1986 or at least since 1984.

8. For the most part we concentrated on the business or enterprise aspects of IG. However, we did include projects (e.g. Welfare) where IG, though not the main aim, was an important factor.

A FRAMEWORK FOR THINKING

THE POSITION OF REFUGEES FOR DEVELOPMENT

Most of this book is designed to help fieldworkers interested in income-generation projects to be able to find quickly the sections relevant to their work. However, in this section, we try to provide the beginnings of a theory to examine refugee situations, as they apply to income-generation. This theory - "Flexible Development" or a developmental approach, within the constraints around refugees who are waiting for durable solutions, will be used throughout the book.

Prior to the mid 1970s, most refugees, except for those in Palestine, were not in one place long enough for development activities to be necessary. Instead, after the emergency/relief phases, the refugees were then able to go on to one of the Three Durable Solutions (See Figure 1.)

Since the mid 1970s, those solutions have become less possible, though they are likely to continue for small numbers of refugees in most cases (see Figure 2.). To simplify the reasons for these changes:

- Repatriation became less likely as the cause(s) for the refugees leaving are still present, such as from Ethiopia and Afghanistan.

- Resettlement for millions of people is on too big a scale for most countries to contemplate and their lack of skills make the majority difficult to integrate into other societies.

- Integration in very poor countries is recognised as being difficult without additional resources. The International Conference on Assistance to Refugees in Africa (ICARA I and II) has seen this and is taking steps to assist host countries, but it is at the start of a long process.

Without these options refugees had to stay longer and move towards a more self-reliant position. If this process towards "flexible development" and away from a relief phase style is allowed, then various forms of income-generation can happen. If not, the refugees become stuck in continuing dependency, which is not good for them or for those trying to help them. Although impossible to simplify, the Palestinian case seems to have remained mainly in the relief phase because of the interrelated reasons of lack of development funds and the political will. However, some income-generating projects have existed or do exist for the Palestinian refugees and, though small in relation to the numbers of refugees, seem to fit the same patterns as in other refugee affected areas covered by this book.

Flexible development has to take into account the relationships between refugees and their hosts, which can vary from a totally separate existance, such as Thailand or Hong Kong, to complete integration like earlier refugees in Tanzania. For the purposes of this manual and the study supporting it, we are concentrating on the area, marked in Figure 2., which is in between these two extremes and which has only arisen since the late 1970s. It varies from refugees in camps that can do some trading to self-settled refugees in towns and cities. It includes all the major refugee populations - in Pakistan, Somalia and the Sudan, as well as many others.

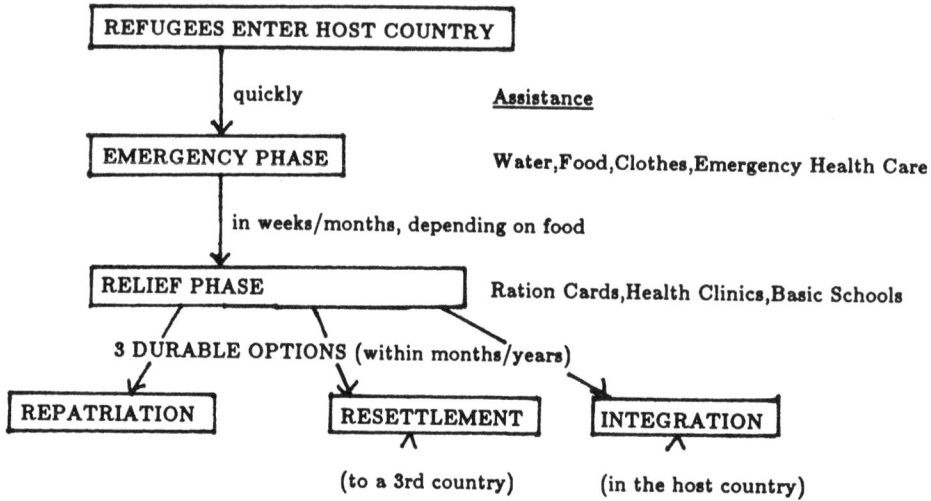

FIGURE 1. Refugees up to mid 1970s

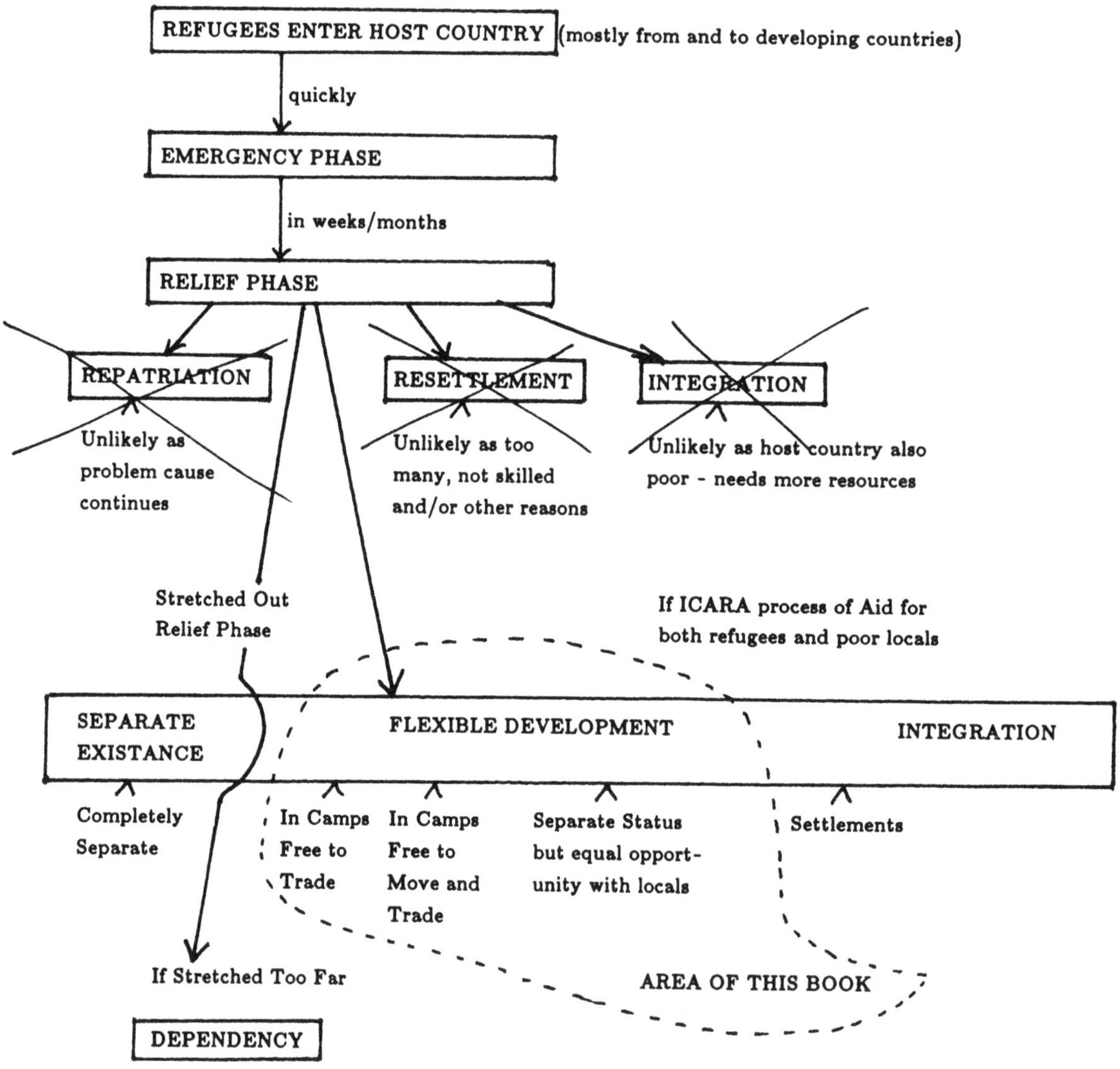

FIGURE 2. Refugees From Mid 1970s

In the flexible development phase all refugee services, such as health, education and so on, become more dependent on the refugees themselves. Many of the relief agencies have gone, or the relief period has finished, leaving only a few trained workers. The refugees want and are expected to be looking more to the future, but within some constraints. If they are in camps, they are constrained by the available land, the opportunities to make and sell. If they are in towns, they have had to learn the language, customs, and laws and accept whatever status is given them. More importantly they do not know their own future - will they return or will they be accepted here? When?

Refugees at this stage will naturally become interested in activities to earn income. But their interest will inevitably be different from that of a local person. They will tend to take a shorter term view, because of the possibility of moving. And, if they can rely on rations, for themselves and their families, then they can also take more risks than a local person. Conversely, if they receive no assistance, their desperation may also increase the risks they are ready to take. It has been said that refugees are psychologically both more conservative and more radical than other people. Conservative, in that they will try to keep their old customs, even if they were losing them in their old country, as a way of retaining their identity. And radical, in that having survived the initial trials of being refugees, they may have a feeling of invulnerability and hence feel able to try anything. Though different in every case, the agency field worker must be aware of the consequences of the particular refugee group's attitudes and not assume they are the same as the attitudes of other refugees or of local people.

Hence the promotion of IG projects for refugees is affected by two sets of problems, which do not necessarily affect similar projects with local people. Firstly, there are the constraints on the refugees set by the "new" conditions in the host country, the environment, the land available, the laws pertaining to refugees, and others. Secondly, there are the refugee attitudes, which may mean an emphasis on training, as with the Afghan refugees who want to prepare for their future, or on self-employment, rather than employment, as an expression of some control over their own lives.

It is in this flexible development phase, while waiting for a longer term solution, that IG programmes can play a large part in helping the refugees determine for themselves the different directions they can take. The agency programmes available for them should increase the options and choices that refugees have. That means that agencies running IG programmes or projects and those supporting or funding them should have a high degree of understanding of both the positive and negative aspects of the refugee situation at the time. Income-generation should not be a last resort: it should be at the forefront of policy.

TYPES AND TIMING OF INCOME GENERATION PROJECTS

As we said earlier the term "income-generation" is a catch-all phrase and is therefore not easily defined. However it is necessary to try to separate out its various parts to understand how it is used. In Figure 3. and in the categories below, we present our attempt, adapted originally from UNHCR Pakistan, to separate out the different types of IG projects. These categories will be used throughout this manual as a way of moving from the question "what now?" to the more specific "what type of IG project is appropriate now?"

The term "project" is taken to mean one assistance package, whereas a "programme" is a group of packages. Hence the Austrian Relief Committee has health and IG programmes in Pakistan. Within the ARC income-generating programme are vocational training, entrepreneur starters and employment bureau projects. This gets complicated when one project has more than one part, such as training, grant and advice components, but in most cases, this split is useful as a starting point for analysis.

Our analysis in Figure 3. goes one step further. Having identified the eight main types of IG project, we suggest that each has its own time-scale, depending on how near it is to the relief phase and also the particular situation in the host country. Some projects can start in the relief phase, others are more developmental, still others can evolve from one to the other.

Though we see a progression to a more self-reliant position, the political situation in the country sets the limits. In Thailand, for instance, the "Humane Deterrence" policy does not allow self-reliance or any integration, although internal camp relief substitution, training for resettlement or self-help activities are allowed. In Pakistan, the tensions of having such a large and relatively skilled refugee population, means that the Government prefers camp based activities to more integrated and therefore competitive ones. In Somalia, the lack of good land and infrastructure reduces the options for integration - unless there is adequate and substantial external assistance. For the agency and the refugee, these are constraints that have to be lived with. However, it must be pointed out, that the economic development of the refugees can benefit the host country and not just the local suppliers of goods.

The following list is a brief introduction to the various types of activities which can be undertaken. Further details are given in sections H. to O. A list of 155 sorts of businesses or projects assisted in the eight categories is given in section P.- which also may help to explain the following categories:

1. RELIEF SUBSTITUTION - Refugees make or grow things to replace "relief" goods such as blankets. They are paid by the relief agency and the goods are then distributed to the refugees.

2. DEVELOPMENT INVESTMENT - These projects aim to provide services, facilities or equipment to assist the development process, rather than helping refugees or refugee businesses directly. There are two types:

    a) Infrastructure - making and maintaining roads, buildings, water
       supply systems, and so on.

b) Environment - Growing trees, making and promoting fuel-saving cookers (as income-saving projects), building dams, erosion walls, and other devices or projects to protect or enhance the environment.

3. INCOME-ADDING STARTERS - Small grants, loans or supplies to start enterprises, which may not provide a whole job or business, but bring in some income now and may expand later - chickens and small gardens are common examples.

4. BASIC SKILL UTILIZATION - Using those skills that the refugees bring with them to the host country. Again there are two main types:

   a) Village Crafts Schemes - Adapting village crafts - items such as handicrafts, baskets, pots, mats - for sale locally or internationally. Often this involves providing raw materials and buying the finished products.

   b) Agricultural Schemes - Starting with traditional knowledge, such schemes can be anything from the simple giving of seeds and a few hand tools to full scale irrigation, marketing, and other assistance. These schemes are very similar to other development schemes not involving refugees and will only be mentioned in this book if there are special aspects relating to refugees. Often these schemes are under a "Refugee Agriculture" section, rather than under "Income-Generation".

5. VOCATIONAL TRAINING/PRODUCTION - Initial training, then gradual conversion to production units, businesses or employment.

6. BUSINESS STARTERS - Making small grants or loans, or giving equipment to refugees to start businesses. This assistance is usually designed to help those with skills return to their previous profession and because of this often omits a detailed business analysis or skills training.

7. BUSINESS ASSISTANCE - Starting after the period of small starter grants or loans, these schemes aim to provide loans and advice on more complex businesses, possibly having technical and marketing assistance.

8. EMPLOYMENT BUREAU - Placing refugees in refugee and local businesses or with refugee agencies.

Although this list of types of IG project clarifies the bewildering number of projects which are all called "income-generating", some further points need to be made before using it:

- Some projects may not fit the categories well, e.g. a craft training project with a starter grant of some equipment could fit three of the types identified above. We feel that a careful study of such projects for their main objective - is it training or is it handicraft or is it an entrepreneur starter? - would classify most IG projects, certainly those in our study.

- One vital question which is not answered by placing a project in one of these categories of IG project is who runs the projects? A handicraft project can be run by one agency, using refugees as workers, or another agency could be supporting refugee handicraft businesses. A training scheme can put on courses for refugees or it could respond to refugees requests as they come up. The former are more in the relief phase, the latter in the developmental phase; we would advocate a gradual move towards the latter style. Indeed for a project to remain agency run does a disservice to the refugees, who can and should take over management whenever possible.

THE TIMING OF REFUGEE INCOME GENERATING PROJECTS

Having identified the eight types of IG projects and the assistance they provide to the refugees, what can be said about the time-scale of introducing and developing them? In Figure 3. on the next page, we suggest there are five intermediate phases as the refugees move from the relief phase to the flexible development phase.

We must remember they are still refugees awaiting one of the durable solutions while in this flexible development phase. However, they are able to contribute to their own lives and to their host countries.

Phase A: During the relief phase, the first steps away from relief should be planned. Such projects need to bring in income, to be capable of being started quickly and must not demand much understanding of the refugee or host cultures - as the personnel involved have not had much time to investigate.

The first three types of IG projects can start at this level:-

Some relief substitution can start by making clothes, blankets or other urgently needed supplies, if the skills and materials are immediately available.

Most development investment such as construction, erosion barriers or planting trees can start quickly employing people in both skilled and more importantly large numbers of unskilled jobs.

Most income adding starters such as giving seeds, tools or chickens can begin the process of encouraging refugees to look to the future, instead of the immediate present.

All these are similar in style to the relief phase of giving things or jobs to the refugees. For development workers, as opposed to those familiar with emergency relief work, this early phase of IG is difficult, as it involves very little self-help on the part of the refugees. However there is some evidence that neither the refugees nor the local population would willingly accept longer term thinking at this phase.

Phase B: Those projects which need a little bit more information can be started. Knowing about the refugees' skills, the available resources and the accessible markets means the refugees' basic skills of farming or crafts can be used. Knowing the differences between their existing skills and the skills needed means that training projects can be designed.

Those projects started in Phase A can be continued, changed or extended as more information becomes available.

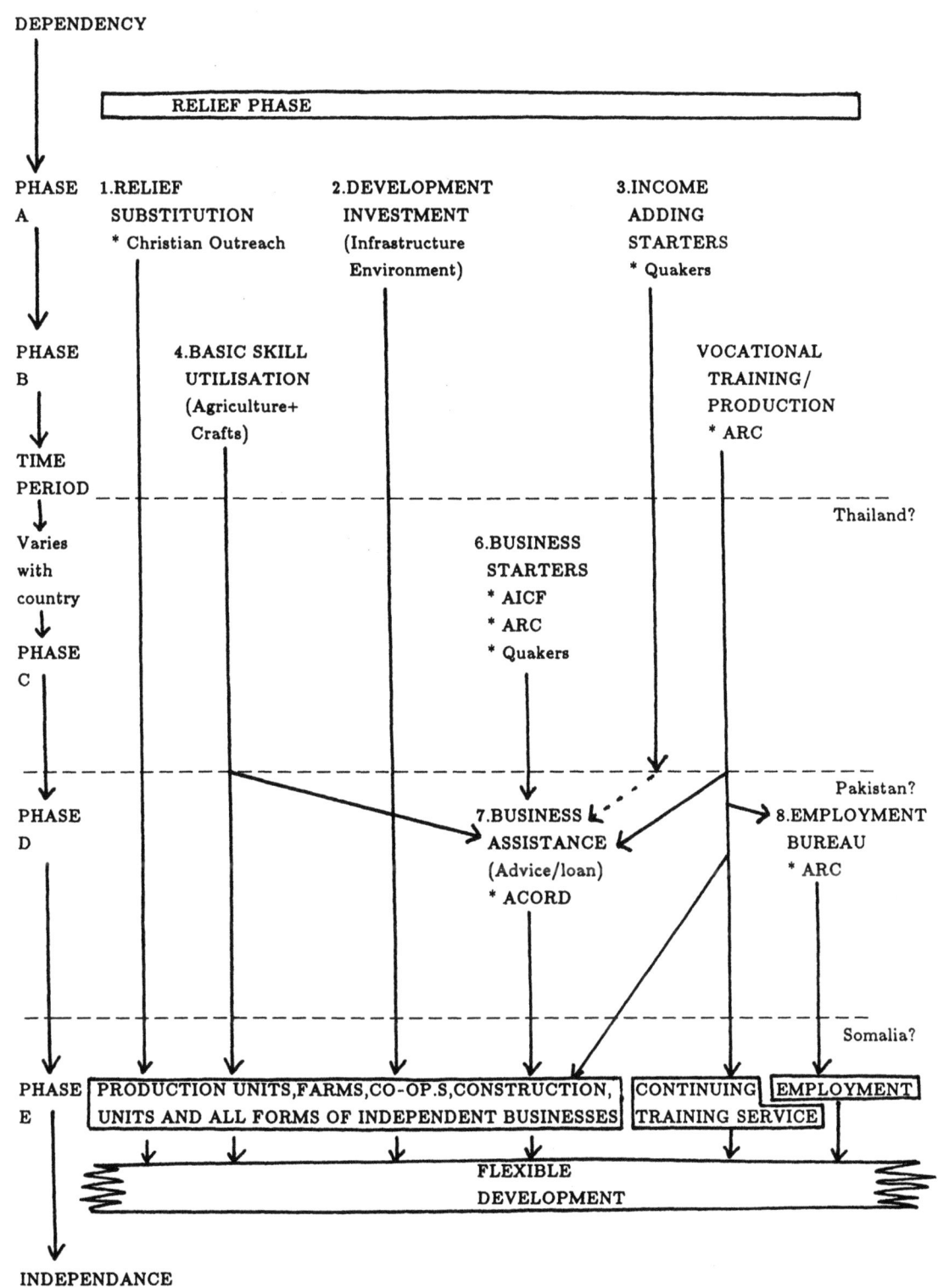

FIGURE 3. Income-generating Projects from Relief to Flexible Development

(* Case study detailed later)

Phase C: This phase is concerned with change. During this phase, it becomes obvious that the refugees will be in the host country for some time. If it is allowed, it is preferable to help refugees begin to do things for themselves, rather than remain unemployed or even employed. Some start by themselves, others with a little starting help can begin their own businesses. These entrepreneurs, particularly if they are not in cities with higher starting costs, can employ themselves, a family member and often someone else for less than $300 capital for each business.

Those IG projects which have already begun in phases A. and B. need to change. Relief substitution projects should start to hand over management and production contracts to the refugees. Farm and village craft projects should move from employment to self-employment. Similarly the development investment projects, dealing with infrastructure and environment, should begin to be run by refugees and/or local people, perhaps becoming independent construction enterprises. The income adding starter projects should be ending as more viable options for businesses become clearer.

Phase D: This phase continues all the changes in phase C., whenever possible moving from agency run to agency assisted projects, from dependency to independence. The Business Starter projects should end and be replaced by a wider range of Business Assistance - advice on marketing and accounting, and loans of bigger amounts, rather than small grants or tool kits to get started.

Phase E: The refugees reach the Flexible Development Phase. They remain refugees, with those constraints, but have independent businesses or are in farms, cooperatives or production units, owned and run by refugees. They are, to some degree, self-supporting and able to contribute to their own and the host countries' economic life.

The time-scale for all these phases is certainly variable and indeed the host country situation may not allow the whole process to be completed. As explained earlier, political constraints may not allow the refugees to go beyond a certain phase.

At the present time (early 1987), the external and internal factors in Thailand mean the refugees there remain in phases A. and B. For Pakistan, competition and the large number of refugees restrict the process to Phase C. In Somalia, the lack of development resources means most of the refugees are at phases C. and D.

This is not to say the situation will always stay the same; there is a dynamic balance between the needs of the host country population and the needs of the refugees. This balance will change with time and other circumstances. There may even be a slight reversal of direction if the local people do not share in the resources given to the refugees. It is the authors' belief that both the refugees and the local population will benefit eventually, if the refugees are both allowed and assisted to become self-sufficient within the development of the whole refugee affected area. Indeed, without encouragement refugees will continue to be dependent upon aid: a situation of little benefit to the refugees, the host country or the international community.

THE POSITION OF REFUGEES AFTER THE RELIEF PHASE

Once the relief phase is over, some agencies leave. The remaining agencies are faced with the dilemma that whereas before everything was set up for the refugees now the feeling is that refugees should do things for themselves. Development agencies are wary - there is no natural "community" to develop, the time-scale and accessible resources are uncertain and psychologically the people are not used to a say in their lives. Nevertheless, some self-settled refugees may have already started to solve these problems for themselves.

Agencies involved in the changeover have few guidelines - let alone rules - on which to base their ideas. Hence the suggestion of "flexible development". It is not durable, in that the situation may change. It is not development in the normal sense - with its implications of community and building a better long-term future in one place. Rather, it is taking people out of dependency to a degree of self-reliance and accepting some constraints.

As far as the agencies are concerned, the split between relief and development is a real one, and even those organizations that have some expertise in both have often allocated the two tasks to different departments. In cases where field directors have responsibility for both, it is rare for them to have experience of both functions or the transition between them. This is partly because it is a relatively new situation and partly because of the differences in outlook between those involved in relief and those involved in development. For relief workers the idea of continuing on for many years is difficult - particularly because they feel they are not "really needed" after the emergency. Some more details of relief type agencies are given in section B.

Those working in development, however, see the intense pressure of relief work and worry about the way it is done - especially if they have to take over and start doing things with and not for the refugees. This is based on a difference in attitudes, but other differences are shown later in sections B. and C. on relief and development agencies. The changeover from relief to development seems most problematic in the area of income-generation. In other areas of assistance the transition seems to be better managed. Health and education workers have, to some extent, already set up their systems to cope with flexible development: there are the agency trainers who hand over to local counterparts and there are manuals in the local language. The field of IG lags behind, possibly because of the political implications such as the use of land, or perhaps because of the change needed in the style of assistance. It must move from developing people, to helping them to develop themselves and allowing them to do so.

Different attitudes seem to be needed at each move away from relief style assistance. In the last section, we suggested that infrastructure, environment, income-adding starters and relief substitution (See the Christian Outreach case study), are suitable for starting, when it is decided by the agency that the relief phase is over. Respondents suggested (from Question B6) this is between six months and two years after the arrival of the refugees in the host country, so planning for these IG projects must start very soon after arrival. This marks the beginning of phase A. The projects all contain a high element of relief or subsidy, but they do ask for some contribution from the refugees.

As the markets and skills available become clearer, the projects involving agriculture (if land is available), training (as in the Austrian Relief Committee case study on p.20) and village crafts start. Although very different, these projects are at the same phase B. and are similar, at least in the sense that the refugees need to make a commitment to staying where they are for a period.

A little later, as it becomes clear what business opportunities are available, the refugees themselves often start shops or other small businesses. Although they rarely help these first businesses, aid agencies' projects often help the next group of entrepreneurs - those who have the potential to start businesses, but need a little assistance. Often help at this point (phase C.) does start the refugee economy and gives an example to others who are hesitant to start. Detailed examples of these business starters are given later in the case studies on the Quakers, ACORD and AICF. There were 33 of the business starter programmes among the 149 IG programmes we studied, making it the second most common type after the 39 training programmes.

In phase D., the business and employment bureaux schemes can start to offer their professional advice. These schemes can only be planned within a relatively stable time-scale and must be based on a good understanding of the political and legal positions of refugees.

In phase E., the refugees run and own their own businesses. They have been able to integrate, at least commercially, with their hosts, even if they have a separate legal status. Many refugees have already reached phase E. informally, without outside assistance or recognition, but they cannot be assisted politically or legally by outside agencies. Since they have got that far without external assistance, they can probably carry on and develop without it. Those refugees who do need help from agencies have probably to remain at the phase allowed in the host country. This may be more true for camp-based refugees, than for those more integrated into the local community.

At each transition between phases a political change and an attitude change are needed. For example, in the transition between phases A. and B. the small farmers or craftsmen or women probably need to be allowed to trade with local people. Something which is not necessary in a relief substitution or development investment project. That legal/political step to allow trade has to happen.

As for the attitude changes, both the refugees and the agencies must accept they are to be in the host country for a period. And that to keep or develop the refugees skills, it means developing trade and production, not more relief. For agencies to assist these businesses, it is counterproductive for one agency to provide everything free and another to ask for a contribution in time or commitment.

At each transition, the attitude and political changes make one more step away from relief and towards development. The same refugees cannot be treated as starving and helpless by one agency and at the same time considered able to help themselves to rebuild their lives by another agency.

CASE STUDIES

In this section, we give five case studies of agencies and their income-generating projects, then a comparison between them. Following that are three case studies of actual refugees and their businesses, then two accounts of "average" refugee businesses generated from the questionnaire data.

ASSISTANCE TO SKILLED REFUGEES - Action International Contre la Faim (AICF) in Pakistan

Main Features of Programme

The AICF income generating project supplies standard tool-kits and other assistance to skilled Afghan refugees. It started after a request from UNHCR in 1984 and a subsequent survey by AICF.

The French AICF team arrived in Pakistan in 1981 and was one of the first agencies to arrive in Baluchistan. AICF started with a Primary Health Care programme and the medical work remains their main activity. The team now feels that their understanding of the culture and the situation of the refugees was more important for success in starting these income-generating activities than previous experience of income-generation in other places.

Background

Since 1978/9, about three million refugees have come to Pakistan and more are arriving. The two provinces of the North-West Frontier with 2.1 million refugees in 244 camps and Baluchistan with 0.6 million refugees in 62 camps have the majority. With the many tribal groupings from each valley in Afghanistan, and the many political groupings, the background is complex, though Islam is a unifying feature.

The women are in "Purdah", which means most stay within their houses and wear a completely covering dress when outside. They had greater freedom in their home villages, but being in camps, which are called refugee villages, next to people they do not know, and in a foreign country, they feel they have to be more careful. Despite this, some of the older women who led the families to Pakistan, have gained a greater respect and authority than they had previously. The Purdah means that although the ratio of men:women:children is nearly normal at 25:28:47, the men are much more accessible and able to work.

It also seems generally accepted that the level of skills posessed by the Afghan refugees and the availability of both materials and products in Pakistan are better than many other refugee areas, like Sudan or Somalia.

The AICF gave assistance to 795 people in 1985, out of 1109 applicants and this created 1129 jobs. They did not give cash, except in very rare cases, for various reasons - both cultural (family money not seen as separate from business money) and political (cash seen as unfair to local people). The average value of the assistance was 2,042 rupees (120 U.S.$), with a range from 400-4,000 rupees and, in total, 54 trades and 53 tribal or clan groups were assisted.

Programme Process

The initial survey provided a full list of possible trades, an idea of the refugees' business needs and the tools needed for each trade. Although these have now been modified by experience and changes in suppliers. AICF chose one field officer, who had been with their medical programme for two years and was "very quick". The rest of the team of five field officers have had varying times with AICF, as six or seven previous field officers have had to be dismissed over the two years of operation - usually for tribal favouritism.

This business starter scheme began in the three biggest camps in Baluchistan, but has since moved on to other camps. Their process varies, but includes the following pattern:

1. A purchase officer buys and keeps stocks of the various tools for the kits, which are different for each trade. AICF buy from several Pakistani suppliers, as one would not keep the stock amount or variety needed.

2. The refugee, preferably, or a relative or a chief (mallik) will approach a field officer and have a preliminary discussion about the scheme. There are also several UNHCR funded training schemes, who pass on the names of trainees who have completed their training. The next stage is for the field officer to go through a comprehensive 25 page questionnaire with the refugee.

3. In doing the questionnaire, the field officer builds up a picture of the person, while looking for the three criteria : a) Are they Skilled? b) Are they Motivated? c) Can the camp and/or the local market absorb the business?

4. Each field officer, all of whom are men, meets the expatriate director every two weeks with his caseload. AICF would like to employ women field officers, but say it is extremely difficult in the Afghani/Pakistani culture. As a result of the discussions some applications are rejected: unmotivated or rich people and those whose close relatives already receive help. If the applicants are needy, such as widowed or disabled, or if their skills are needed, such as well-diggers, then they are usually acccepted.

About 70% of applicants' incomes are under 100 U.S.$ per month, which indicates that the kits are going to the poorest. The rejections are made mostly for the reasons that either there is a saturated market or that there is no demand for that business.

5. The accepting of the grant of the kit is witnessed, though no contract is signed. Only 12 businesses have failed and, with pressure from the malliks who still maintain their traditional power, all the tools have been returned. The kits are provided to 96% of those accepted, 8% get a grant of rent for business premises for a period and 3% get raw materials. These latter are difficult to reclaim in the event of a failure and so are only provided in rare cases.

6. In some cases, when the kits are not ready, the applicants are put on a waiting list and have to wait for a short period, on average two months.

7. Sometimes the field officers will also give business advice, for example on siting or marketing, which they can do through experience rather than training. They keep a close eye on the market, especially on saturation levels for each trade, to answer the question as to whether the area can the area absorb the business.

8. When one camp nears saturation, then the field officers move on to the next. This saturation is indicated visually by the numbers of businesses having AICF signposts - about 75% of the businesses put up the signposts. Or saturation can be shown by reducing incomes from competition between businesses of the same type, such as tailors. By November 1986, AICF had covered about 50% of the camps/refugee villages in Baluchistan.

9. All the participants are monitored after two months and occasionally after that. It has been found that six per cent leave the business for personal reasons and less than one per cent for other reasons, giving one indication that the scheme is working as designed.

RESULTS/EVALUATION

This IG scheme seems to rely on the expatriate director and his field officers, with their knowledge and experience of the culture to provide a very effective project for the skilled refugees. They admit it is very difficult for them to help the unskilled, or the agriculural sector, or women; these groups make up only 4% of those assisted.

The main trades are tailors 15%, carpenters 13%, welldiggers 11%, shoe repairers 6%, 5% each for masons, bicycle repairers, cooking stove repairers and carpet weavers. The remaining 45 trades are all less than 4% with 20 trades having only one person assisted - trades such as a juicemaker, a photographer, a bucket maker and others.

FINANCIAL DETAILS

For 1987, the budget will be:

	U.S. $
Wages (about half will be expatriate-related costs, the local field officers will be paid about $200 per month)	54,000
Administration (office, rent, transport and travel)	16,000
Assistance (costs of kits, rents or raw materials provided)	280,000
Total (for about 1,200 businesses)	350,000

Previous budgets were similar, though the cost of the actual assistance given was about half this, mainly because the average cost of kits was half the maximum grant allowed in the budget. The final figures for 1985/6 were not completed at the time of the study, but using the information available in this case study and adding that there was a slightly higher administrative cost for the initial supplies, such as motorbikes for the field officers, then :

	U.S. $
Wages and administration (slightly higher than above)	75,000
Assistance cost - 795 businesses x $120 (no rent/materials)	95,400
Total cost	170,400
Cost per business (795 businesses)	214
Cost per job (1129 jobs)	151

The administrative cost is kept low by sharing overheads with the medical programme and no figure is included for the stock of tools bought.

Comments

1. The knowledge built up in the very different field of the medical programme enabled the Director and the first Field Officer, without previous knowledge of income-generating projects, to start a small scheme which grew into the present very comprehensive project.

2. The relative availability of local resources and skilled refugees enabled a high take-up and a high rate of success for the businesses.

3. The way in which other agencies' training programmes in send their trainees into the AICF scheme has shown that a mutually beneficial planning and coordination process is taking place between agencies.

EXPANDING OUT OF RELIEF - The Austrian Relief Committee in Pakistan

Main Features of Programme

Early in 1980, the UNHCR and the Pakistan Government asked the Austrian Relief Committee (ARC) for help with health services, as the most urgent need for the influx of Afghan refugees. Since then the health programme of ARC has been involved with curative medical care (over 30,000 cases in 1985), training community health workers and traditional birth attendants, and running a sanitation programme. ARC have expanded into projects giving basic business starting assistance to skilled refugees, a multi-purpose training centre, and an employment bureau. They have also assisted with many small, one-off activities, such as publishing a story book and translations of "Where there is no Doctor" in local languages, and helping 51 especially needy refugees.

Background

At the beginning of the emergency, an Afghan-born Austrian citizen, who had spent ten years in Austria, firstly as a student, then as an electrical engineer, returned with the ARC to help the Afghan refugees. To gain acceptance into the strong Afghan culture, he lived with the refugees for six months (see the previous AICF casestudy for more details on Afghan refugees). His backround has given strength to the running of this variety of projects and his advice has been helpful to many agencies. There is a lot of collaboration between ARC and outside organizations and ARC is itself funded by thirteen agencies from six countries.

The Multi-Purpose Technical Training Centres (MPTTC) began in early 1983. A sewing project, which started in late 1983, was transferred to a Danish organization in April 1985. The Assistance to Skilled Afghan Refugees (ASAR) began in August 1984 and is continuing. An Employment Bureau, which started after many discussions in November 1985 had to close in Autumn 1986. These form the main income-generating parts of the ARC programme.

In the autumn of 1986 several bombings in Pakistan and the growth of Afghan run businesses within Pakistan of up to 25% in some business sectors (even more in transportation), combined with the return of Pakistani expatriates from the Gulf States to cause political difficulties. These resulted in a Pakistan Government request to confine the aid more to the refugee villages and thus avoid increased resentment by the local population towards the refugees. One of the casualties of this understandable slight change in Pakistan's generous assistance to the worlds biggest influx of refugees, was the closure of the ARC Employment Bureau. The Bureau was situated in Peshawar, the capital of the North-West Frontier Province (NWFP) and holding the biggest refugee population. It is to ARC's credit that they adapted quickly and are continuing to expand with their motto "Help Refugees Help Themselves."

Programme Process

A. ASAR

The assistance programme to skilled refugees started as a pilot project in the last half of 1984. The 1985 programme was designed out of this, with the following process:

1. Surveying: As each area or group of refugee camp villages is completed, that is when most of the requests have been supplied, then a new area is surveyed. In each survey the elders and other camp representatives are visited and asked for a list of the names of potential skilled refugee participants. In the first area, the ARC staff also had many discussions with the refugees to get information on the appropriate style and sorts of assistance for each trade.

2. Identification: The refugees on the list are interviewed and have to go through a long verbal discussion, with standard proformas (questionnaires) for their theoretical and practical skills. If they pass, they become eligible for assistance. In 1985, 1,243 refugees were interviewed and 1,107 accepted by the four field staff.

3. Market Research and the Purchase of Tools: In the initial market research to assess the different refugee trades, the two research officers of ARC found 67 different trades, 60 of which were considered feasible and socially desirable and therefore eligible. A weapons trader for instance would not be eligible. The Purchase Officer then buys the tools as required in bulk from Pakistani town suppliers and kits are made up for each trade, for 53 trades so far. This "First Phase Assistance" is up to a maximum of 4,000 rupees (U.S.$237) with an average of 2,000 rupees.

4. Distribution of the tools: In 1985, the ARC staff returned to most of the 1107 refugees who had been accepted to give out the tool kits for the requested trade. They gave tools to 608 men and 308 women. A further 124 had been accepted and were eligible, but not at the distribution. Another 67 could not be reached in 1985, because of lack of permission to visit or the onset of the cold season. Some camps are in dangerous border areas or are in the mountains with snow over winter. ARC have covered some camps in most districts in NWFP and intend to cover a total of about 200 camps. Their target is to assist 140 refugees a month.

5. First Phase Monitoring: One month after giving the assistance, the field officers and one technical advisor return to the refugees to give advice and check for further needs. If a refugee qualifies for this second phase assistance (and only ten per cent do), then he or she can receive up to a total value of 6,000 rupees, including the first phase assistance.

6. Second Phase monitoring: After six months, the field officers return to give the final technical and managerial help and do an evaluation. In the future ARC hope to add more managerial assistance at this point.

B. MPTTC
Before starting the Multi-Purpose Technical Training Centres , a detailed survey was undertaken with camp authorities, elders and a representative sample of 169 refugees to find out what sort of training was required.

There is one centre in Peshawar (which may be moved to the refugee villages for the political reasons given above) and one centre in a camp, which is just getting started. The centre in Peshawar has run courses in welding, machine work, electrics, auto-repair and auto-service. They also ran a general technical course and basic courses in literacy, numeracy, first aid, English and religion. These basic courses are available to other agencies. Some of the trainees' production is used by the ARC medical teams. In 1985, 130 refugees were trained and the target for 1986 is 200.

C. EBAR
The Employment Bureau ran succesfully for nearly a year to the end of October 1986 and placed 120 qualified Afghan Refugees in jobs, especially in the various aid agency programmes.

Results/Evaluation
ARC is always looking for new ways to assist. Through the ASAR project, ARC found various new needs: to help bigger businesses that need more than one person, or to give assistance exceeding the limit of 6,000 rupees. This they plan to do with a hire purchase component rather than cash, which runs the danger of being thought of as like free "rations" and therefore used as the family sees fit, rather than for the specified business. The giving of cash could also lead to further resentment by the local Pakistani population.

ARC are also concerned about the negative aspects of just "giving" aid and hope to introduce interviewing charges for ASAR and MPTTC, as well as other techniques to increase participation and involvement. They accept that only 10-15% of the population are enterprising enough to take advantage of these projects and are worried about the rest, who are mostly from farming backrounds and who are not active and need some other form of assistance.

In all their projects ARC are aware of a degree of unfairness in that the refugees are getting aid and the very similar local population are not. Most of their donors have agreed this year to Parallel Funding, for similar schemes run on dual lines for refugees and local people - if such schemes can be devised. As mentioned earlier, this dual approach is needed as there is growing Pakistani resentment over the issue.

For ASAR about 75% of the skilled refugees are using the assistance kit fully, the majority practising their trade to some extent. For those not making full use of the assistance provided, the main problems are the:

- limited access to the market, which is likely to continue.
- need for further capital in the start-up stage.
- lack of infra-structure, such as electricity supply.
- lack of managerial experience.
- other social or cultural responsibilities - especially domestic duties for women.

For the training centre MPTTC, of the 130 refugees trained in 1985 :

- 22 are in ARC supervised workshops, a form of half-way stage between training and owning their own workshops. They have to pay back a starting loan.
- 6 are continuing as "master trainees" in the Centre.
- 20 are employed.
- The remaining 82 need tools, capital, a workshop and a supervisor to carry on their trade. ARC are working hard to improve this situation, perhaps with combinations of the above solutions.

Financial Details
ARC's total budget is about 20 million rupees (1.2 million U.S.$), of which about half is spent on the income-generating schemes. In the IG programme:
- 16% is staff salaries and wages.
- 76% on refugee materials, equipment or stipends.
- 8% on transport and administrative costs.

On the basis of the present figures available, the authors calculate that ASAR costs about $200-300 per job, and the Technical Training Centre MPTTC costs about ten times this sum per training place.

Comments

1. ARC have demonstrated great flexibilty in evolving and developing appropriate solutions to the changing refugee needs, especially when no previous experience was available. ARC carried out much of the experimenting, which others have followed.

2. The main advantage has been the excellent cultural understanding; other agencies in Pakistan were quick to mention insights they obtained from ARC.

3. ARC are constantly re-evaluating their programme and adjusting it to changing circumstances.

4. The Afghan refugees themselves realize their situation is not short term and are actively looking for assistance based on this longer term perspective. They prefer, for example, to choose better courses, most likely to gain them employment, with no stipends, rather than other training courses with stipends. This showed in the MPTTC training project.

5. The coordination factor is important for the Austrian Relief Committee in Pakistan and they have tried hard to cooperate on projects with other agencies.

AFTER RELIEF WHAT? Quakers in Somalia

Main Features of Programme

The Quaker programme began in July 1982, three years after the first refugees entered Somalia. It was and is a camp-based community development programme, concentrating on IG, though there is some extension work into the local area.

The first projects were with two income-adding starters - chickens (for women), gardens (mostly for men) and also some school projects. After one year, a more advanced business starter project was initiated, with some elements of business advice. By July 1985, the business project comprised about one third of the work; with three small garden projects taking another third; and other projects, mainly appropriate technology projects, such as donkey carts, fuel-saving cookers, hand-powered grain grinders and water pumps, making up the remaining portion.

The two income-adding starters and the business starter projects are described below.

Background

In 1979/80 over one million refugees entered Somalia from Ethiopia. Some settled themselves, but most went into thirty-five refugee camps. Both the American and British Quakers (American Friends Service Committee and Quaker Peace and Service) are religious based organizations and they cooperated to investigate and then implement this flexible programme.

It was started, after several exploratory visits, when it was judged to be the right time to move from relief towards development. The authors Chris and Clare Rolfe, who had community development backgrounds in England, were sent to Daray Macaane, a camp in North-West Somalia, where the refugees had shown a degree of initiative by starting to build schools and shops on their own. The camp itself was in a hilly region, six kilometres from the local town of Boroma. Both camp and town had similar populations of between twenty and forty thousand people, and were mostly from a similar ethnic group, with many refugees having local relatives.

A. CHICKEN PROJECT

Programme Process

As one of the initial projects, this had two main objectives: a) to help the refugees to supplement their income and improve their nutrition.and b) to help the programme gain acceptance in the camp while learning about the refugees, their needs and organizations. During fifteen months of operation and later evaluations the project developed in the following way:

1. In initial discussions with the camp authorities and refugee representatives, it became clear that both parties were expecting aid to be given in the same way that food, clothes, tents, and other things had been given up to that time. It was also clear that the refugees wanted chickens. The authors had expected to have time to learn about the cultural background and study the needs of the refugees, but this was not to be because both the refugees and authorities demanded action from the start.

2. The team therefore agreed to start a poultry project and built in some other objectives - the chicken project would work with a total of twenty-four groups in the six poorest sections of the camp. This would give the Quaker team some knowledge of group processes and some more intensive knowledge of how the poorest were living in the camp.

3. As the team had only a little experience of chickens, other projects in Somalia were visited. These projects used the only available imported bird, the White Leghorn, which produced a large number of eggs, but often died under camp conditions. It was decided to cross-breed this bird and the local chickens, the aim being to breed birds which gave more eggs and did not die. Six prime Leghorn cockerels were brought to the camp from the government farms which were three hours drive away, and sixty prime hens were bought in the local town of Boroma. The cockerels and hens were then separated equally into two farms, in case disease hit one of the farms.

4. While the cross-breeding was proceeding, the team had several discussions to try and identify the poorest groups - as "we all are" was the usual reply to the question "who is the poorest?" The groups, with ten women in each, were administrative groups, that collected rations together. The final twenty-four groups chosen were visited and those which agreed to build the chicken houses and attend a series of five lessons, were promised twenty cross-breed chicks (eighteen hens and two cockerels).

5. Given the low egg production of the local hens, the cross-breeding process was slow. The use of an incubator was unfortunately stopped by an accidental fire. But this slow speed enabled more detailed group discussions to occur and the lessons to be improved and spread out. The five lessons covered housing, feeding, disease, breeding and cooking of both eggs and chickens. All the lessons were taught in Somali and all the materials, recipes and other inputs were local.

Results/Evaluation
Of the 480 chickens given out about two-thirds survived a big predator problem, which included foxes, mongeese, civets, hawks and cats. About another hundred cross-breed cockerels were swopped for local cockerels, in any condition, to improve the local stock and to use in the cooking lessons. The refugees chosen did appear to be the poorest as only a few had raised chickens before.

The lessons also proved successful: two years after the project more white chickens are still around the camp and the town, with the area becoming well known for its good poultry. The team gave no assistance in building the chicken houses, apart from advice. Though the refugees wanted items such as chicken wire, the Quaker team produced designs using stone and sticks, and thus avoided the problem of importing materials, which could stop the refugees building more chicken houses, unless external assistance is provided.

Only one third of the groups of ten women decided to keep their chickens collectively, the rest of the groups preferred to reallocate the chickens individually. Comparing this to the womens' garden project, it seems that where it is practical projects should be aimed at individuals - individual women can look after chickens, but not gardens. This is a valuable point in deciding to avoid future group projects.

Financial Details

	U.S.$
This project cost approximately:	
For all the chickens, equipment, supply and transport	5,000
For the expatriate volunteer for two thirds of a year, including all associated costs	4,000
For the Somali and refugee staff at exchange rates then	4,000
For administration - a proportion of total other costs	1,000
Total =	14,000

With 230 participants (one group of 10 dropped out), this gives a cost per person of $61. In terms of benefit to the refugees, the worst valuation would be given if all the chickens were sold, and the best if the hens were kept and the eggs sold:

	U.S.$
Worst Case	
320 chickens that survived @ $11 each =	3,520
100 cocks swopped @ $11 equivalent each =	1,100
Total =	4,620
Best Case:	
If the eggs and cockerels were sold:	
3 Sh/egg, 15 eggs/month, 9 months/year, 16 Sh/ U.S.$, for 320 hens =	8,100
100 cockerels @ $11 =	1,100
Total =	9,200

Most chickens were used to lay eggs to sell, so if a median value of nearly $7,000 is taken, the project paid for itself after two years.

B. HOUSE GARDEN PROJECT

From the same discussions with camp authorities and refugee representatives that started the chicken project, it emerged that up to 75% of the adults in the camp had been semi-nomads and had done some maize or sorghum farming and that many refugees had very small gardens around their huts. The team offered possible help with seeds and tools, but again built in some other social objectives. The first objective was to help two good gardeners in each of the twenty-four sections. Then these refugees would help another two refugees in their section begin to garden, giving a total of ninety-six gardeners. The team would then be able to have a little knowledge of each section and of individual and group cooperation. It was not specified whether the participants should be men or women.

1. First, the section leaders were visited, told in more detail about the project and asked to choose the four people in each section. They chose ninety-three men and three women; several of the men later proved only to want the tools and did not want either to garden or to help others.

2. The first eight sections were visited and intensively questioned about their needs, which were 1) land, 2) tools, 3) seeds, 4) water and 5) advice in that order. Most of the gardeners found or extended a piece of land of an average fifty square metres. The Quakers provided locally made tools and imported those not made locally. A wide range of vegetable seeds was also imported to try. There were no local shops selling seeds or imported tools.

Most farmers had grown cereals, but had not grown many vegetables before. However, vegetables were chosen as the focus of the project because they were better for the available land, for selling and for nutrition. Jerry cans or shared donkeys were given to help lift the water up the hills. An experienced refugee farmer and a part-time local agricultural student gave advice.

3. The other sixteen sections turned out to be similar and over the year's operation much was learned about methods, preferred crops, etc. This information enabled two more projects to be started:

> 1. a womens' gardening project, using shared gardens, because the women all had other responsibilities and could not garden full-time.

> 2. a garden training project focussing on preferred plants, better spacing and seed multiplication to obtain bigger yields and more income, without further assistance.

Evaluation

About half the gardeners continued cultivating their gardens, but they did not cooperate with one another as had been planned. Although the project failed in this respect, it at least provided a valuable lesson. The chicken project confirmed this fact. Thereafter, assistance was mainly aimed at individuals rather than groups, and this applied particularly to the business project.

The section leaders' choices of people did not follow the criteria given, so although they were always consulted, they were not asked to choose participants again. Rather, projects were designed so that refugees could join in if they were interested.

Over this project period, the area in the camp under cultivation increased from about five to about eight hectares. At each harvest a farmer could make an average profit of 10,000 shillings (then about $600). The varieties of vegetables grown increased from an average of four to an average of eleven.

Financial Details

This project cost approximately: U.S.$
    For the tools, seeds and equipment   6,000
    For the same other costs as the chicken project   9,000
    Total =   15,000

With 96 participants, this gives a cost of $156 per person.

In terms of benefit, since only half the 96 participants worked: 48 refugees at an average of $600 per year = nearly $29,000 (not counting the value of tools, etc.).

In financial terms this project paid for itself in just under six months.

C. SMALL BUSINESS LOAN AND ADVICE SCHEME

In August 1983 the Quaker team had begun to think about helping businesses in the camp, when a UNHCR team came to the camp to disburse loans. There were about one hundred applications, but only two loans were given, as the fund was small and covered all ten camps in the North.

The Quaker team had not run business projects before and there were no other similar projects in Somalia to learn from, though one in Kenya (Partnership for Productivity) gave some advice. So the initial project design was mostly based on an understanding of the camp, rather than on business expertise.

To start to cope with the raised expectations an initial experiment for ten businesses was agreed by December 1983 with the refugee authorities and UNHCR. The business advisor was employed in January and the first loans given in March 1984. In June the scheme was extended as it had already reached eighteen businesses. By July 1985 the scheme had given fifty-one loans - with each month an average of four new businesses starting repayments and four existing loans ending. The scheme continues with a new team, having had about four hundred applications. The refugees went through the following process:

1. A refugee came to the Quaker camp office with or without a written application. One of the Somali community workers discussed the idea with him or her, within the limits of the following criteria:

   a) A maximum loan of 10,000 Shillings per person (The Official Exchange Rate went from sixteen Sh/$ to eighty Sh/$, but the black market rate changed from forty to eighty Sh/$ in the eighteen month period). In 1985, the limit was increased to 15,000 Sh, reflecting the equivalent increase in local prices.

   b) The businesses to last longer than 12 month (maximum loan time) period.

   c) The team preferred businesses which were:

   - "Productive" (some shops and stalls were already set up and loans to others would have led to unfair competition, unless there was a special need). Most of the rejections were shops.

   - Of benefit to town and camp, not just the camp.

   - Individuals or cooperatives - the project did not approve loans to applicants who proposed either to employ others in an exploitative way or not to be fully employed themselves. As a result, all the loans were to individuals or cooperatives.

2. There were usually several subsequent discussions with the community worker, until the applicants had a good general proposal for a loan or did not return. In two special cases, grants were given to newly arrived refugees, but these were very small and only given because they had not had years in the camp to build a security/guarantee. They were checked later and their businesses were found to be successful.

3. The community worker then introduced the applicant(s) and the proposal to the business advisor, who went through the proposal, preparing a simple analysis form (see copy in section U.) of the loan, repayment and estimated income and costs. This was later made more precise by both the applicants and business advisor by checking the costs and the possible market. For instance, the business advisor found the market for tailoring was saturated after six loans to tailors - the existing tailors began to have spare time in the working day.

This process again could take several meetings. On average a successful proposal took one month from the initial meeting to getting a cheque. In some cases small experimental loans were approved to test the market if no examples existed (e.g., ghee making), with the scheme accepting the risk.

4. When a final analysis form had been completed, the expatriate staff discussed the application with both the local staff and the applicants. Again, sometimes more discussions and checking were necessary.

5. On reaching a satisfactory application, a simple agreement was drawn up (see this form and another example in section U.) and checked with the camp administration for their approval of the business and the applicants. This checking provided a safeguard: the guarantee was any combination of returning the equipment provided, some collateral, such as a cow, or a guarantor pledging money if the business failed, these together made up the value of the loan. Only one person was refused, a radio repair man, because his business was not felt to be a camp need.

6. The agreement was signed by the applicants, one of the Quaker workers and the camp commander. Five agreement copies, including two for the police and the court. The latter two made this condition - to get copies on signing, which meant they acted as part of the security and could later be involved in the loan recovery.

7. A cheque was given to the applicant or to the main members if it was a cooperative. The business advisor then took them to the local town bank, where they received their money and were told how to pay back - at the bank into the Quaker Business Account, starting in two months time and then every month.

8. Follow-up meetings with the advisor took place as necessary, from as many as three times a week to once a month. Notes of these meetings were written down and gone through in supervision and training sessions between the advisor and one of the team coordinators.

9. If a payment was not made into the bank at the end of the month, then the business advisor followed up quickly in person. This helped to prevent more complex problems from developing.

Evaluation

OBJECTIVE 1 - The first objective was to provide a business loan and advice service in Daray Macaane. Fifty-one businesses, involving ninety-one men and thirty-six women, started with loans and the two new refugee groups, with eight men, mentioned earlier had grants. Sixteen of these business loans were to groups, the rest to individuals.

List of Small Business Advice and Loan Scheme Businesses:

7 bakers of various breads, sweets, cakes, and pancakes
6 tailors
5 traditional pot or mat makers (these had to be special in some way
    as most people knew how to make the basic types)
5 wood sellers
3 meat selling groups (the loans enabled the groups to buy large animals,
    such as camels, which could easily be cut into pieces of meat as small
    as 100g, whereas before the loan, they could only buy small animals,
    like goats, and these could only be cut into large and therefore
    expensive pieces)
3 charcoal-making groups
3 sisal-processing groups (for ropes, mats and beds)
3 shoe makers
2 lime cooperatives (limestone is burnt to produce a simple cement)
2 stone cutting groups (for building)
2 chicken farmers (not very succesful - feed and predators make this
    very difficult in the camp with more than a few birds)
2 kerosene sellers (none before in camp, all was brought from town)
1 each of: barber, donkey cart operator, irrigation pipe for a farmer, drink seller, gheemaking group, brick-making group, tool-making group and a tie-dye cooperative (this last received more intensive support, as a business new to N.W. Somalia)

OBJECTIVE 2 - The second objective was to provide loan capital in a revolving fund for businesses. Nearly 470,000 Somali shillings was disbursed in loans, which was worth about $12,000 at the then exchange rates. An average loan was 8,600 Sh (excluding the loan to the Tie-dye business of 30,000 Sh). The lowest loan was for 3,150 Sh to a traditional pot maker, and the highest was to the stone cutters' cooperative for 23,670 Sh.

During the eighteen months there was a continuous drought, which made business conditions very tough for everybody, not only those involved in agriculture. The tool makers, for instance, could not sell agricultural tools. The Somali shilling devaluation by 400% over the period, caused problems for those business people relying on imported items, such as tailors who imported cloth. And there was also a cholera epidemic, which led to a ban on all movement for two months and then further restrictions.

There was therefore a lot of loan rescheduling, but despite this 53% of possible payments were made. Two businessmen ran away (one gave money to family, the other tried smuggling) and two businessmen were bad repayers. Ten businesses did not need to reschedule, the other thirty-seven reached agreements to reschedule, and repaid as arranged.

OBJECTIVE 3 - This was to provide grants of up to 50% to businesses which required experimentation, were new to the area, or were more risky for other reasons. In starting this business scheme, it was felt that it would be more successful and certainly less time consuming to the Quaker staff to use people's existing skills. So the only example of this objective was the tie-dye business (30,000 Sh grant and 30,000 Sh loan), which involved sending eight young women (three from the town) to the capital Mogadishu for training. The continuous training in skills and management, did indeed take a lot of staff time, but this was seen as acceptable, because of its wider objective of import substitution.

OBJECTIVE 4 - This was: In the future to make the scheme as independent as possible. The problems of supply, inflation and drought took priority over preparing local structures for take-over, making this objective a priority for the next coordinators.

Financial Details

Over the eighteen months the costs were:	U.S.$
The loan capital for the 51 businesses	12,000
One third time for the expatriate volunteer	3,000
Local staff costs (reduced by devaluation)	1,000
Transport, administrative and other costs	2,000
Total =	18,000

With the 127 participants and 51 businesses, this gives rough figures of $140 per job and $350 per business, including the four failures and not adjusting for the devaluation. Normally, the loan capital would not be considered a cost, as it would be reused, but because of the rescheduling, the devaluation, and since the agency does not recover the loan, it seemed fairer to treat it as a cost in these comparisons.

The income to each refugee was on average 20% of the loan amount per month - remembering that all the loans were worked out on the analysis form for one month, and these were checked later during the visits of the business advisor.

The worst case would be that only the 53% who repaid the loans during the drought and other difficulties actually received this income:

A total of 20% x $12,000 x 12 months x 53% success = $15,264
The "payback" time would be about fourteen months.

There is reason to believe, by doing the rescheduling, that the real success rate is between 80-90%. If an assumption is made that the refugee business people continued paying themselves, though not the project, during the rescheduled period, this gives an income of:

20% x $12,000 x 12 months x 85% success = $24,480
The "payback" time would be about nine months.

All these attempts at quantitative comparisons of costs and benefits are clearly very approximate, but they do give a rough asssesment of the relative economic merits of such IG schemes. And they demonstrate that the project gives greater benefits to the participants, than if the money had just been given them as cash. Such schemes provide continuing benefits for no further cost, unlike pure relief projects.

Comments

1. Knowledge of the camp - these first two income-adding starters, the chicken and the first garden project, enabled much better planning of later projects. The expatriate coordinators actually lived in the camp and this meant that problems could be dealt with promptly. For instance, this enabled the use of very simple forms as all parties were in the camp or town. Any dispute could be followed up quickly with the backing of the authorities, and there was no need for over-legal documents - as would be necessary for projects giving loans, but without close contact with their beneficiaries or local authorities.

2. Not for the poorest - The programme consistently strove to work with the poorest refugees in the camp, and the three local community workers, one man and two women - one of whom was a refugee, often went out into the camp to try and improve the access to the projects. However, the poorer people usually had lower skill levels and less available time, which meant the programme had to find ways of increasing their available time and then train them. This proved difficult and an acceptable process was never found, but thinking continues on this.

3. Not for the richest - we had several requests for lorries, hotels, diesel irrigation pumps and grain grinders. We tried to refer these to other agencies if we felt they were feasible, but none were taken up. As the only non-medical expatriate agency in the area, and as representatives of the rich "Northern" countries, these requests were understandable.

4. Not primarily an employment scheme - all the projects were designed for the refugees to continue the activities started, not just to create income. Even the employed staff numbers were kept low, at ten or less, to keep the agency input as low as possible, so the refugees would not depend on them. Hence the main objective was not employment, and this showed when, under the loan scheme, some refugees came with ideas for businesses to employ others and were refused loans. These applicants were refused because either the proposed businesses were exploitative or the applicants did not have the technical and managerial skills and experience needed. This latter lack of skills might have been because such refugees were already in the local town.

5. Future of the Loan/Advice Project - extensions were planned into more "new" businesses, poorer people, more training and into the local non-camp area, as well as making the projects more Somali run. The latter would be the most difficult as no loan interest was charged - the project was started when it was difficult socially/politically to ask refugees to pay anything for aid. With no income from fees, charges or interest, the problem of covering the costs for local staff and running costs and inflation needs to be overcome. Somalia is the sixth poorest country in the world and any government or local group would be unlikely to take over without continuing aid. With aid, these projects seem a very cost-effective way of moving some refugees and/or local people towards self-sufficiency. However, the question of ending rations for the refugee business people was never asked and could well be counter-productive.

6. Advantages of this camp - Daray Macaane is situated near a big town which has contacts with an international port (Djibouti). It is a long way from the capital and this may make experimentation easier, as negotiations can take place at the local level, without added bureaucracy. 90% of the local people and the refugees were from the same clan, so there was little friction. The local authorities, such as the bank, police and others, were very helpful, perhaps because of the regular contact with the agency over the three years.

7. Disadvantages - devaluation, drought and cholera have already been mentioned. The land is also extremely poor, supporting mostly nomads, a little shifting agriculture during the rains, and a very small area of irrigated land next to dry river beds where water flows reliably underneath the surface all year.

In the local town, there is no medium or large scale industry and cottage industry skills, such as blacksmithing and pottery are very basic and low caste. This imposes great limitations - the market for anything gets saturated quickly, for example the six tailors were the all the camp could support. Hence it is always necessary to use the refugees' skills and to keep looking for new resources and markets, in any and every direction.

THE BUSINESS END - ACORD in Port Sudan

Main Features of Programme
The original idea of the programme was to integrate refugees into the informal business sector of a rapidly expanding town with a mixed population of half a million. It was soon realized that this was discriminatory: the poor in Port Sudan were in exactly the same situation as the refugees. So the poorest of the town became the focus, with the programme assisting refugees (30%), women (40%) and other disadvantaged getting special attention. A deliberate social mix of staff was chosen to provide advice, technical assistance and to supply sheltered workspace, marketing outlets, hire purchase, short term loans and microcredit. It is run on a very business-like basis, charging some costs and fees for its services.

Background
Over one million refugees and displaced persons have been on the move in Sudan. And the city of Port Sudan, on the Red Sea, acts as a magnet for many - it is expanding at 9% a year! 75% of the population are below the poverty line (over 90% of income is spent on food). About 13% are refugees.

ACORD, which is changing its name from EuroAction Acord, was formed from a consortium of agencies in Europe and now includes some Canadian agencies. It focussed initially on development in the Sahel and already had an agricultural settlement programme for refugees in Sudan, but had not had an Urban programme before. To investigate such a programme, ACORD sent in a husband/wife couple with a flexible brief in May 1982 - they spent thirteen months preparing, then the programme started in June 1984.

Programme Process
Five teams of advisors, usually two men and two women work in the poorest areas of the town. The programme is now collectively managed by its staff, with an expatriate coordinator. The process for their loans and advice is as follows:

1. There are five sub-offices, based in the poorer districts and each advertises its services by visits, notices and word of mouth, when the current case load allows.

2. An applicant is charged a registration fee (£S2) after the following criteria and conditions are explained and agreed and the first home visit is planned:

   a) They must be members of a Port Sudan household and contributing to its income or its activities.

   b) Their household income should not be more than £S80 per head per month.

   c) The applicant should have been a resident of Port Sudan for more than 2 years.

   d) The applicant must accept the following conditions:
      i) A full household survey
      ii) Pay an consultancy fee of £S1-5, as appropriate.
      iii) If a loan is agreed a charge of 1% of total value per month,
         is made for administrative costs.
      iv) A fine of £S5 for late payers.

   e) Refugees, women and disabled are given priority by ACORD. The Sudanese authorities do not allow licenses to any more hawkers, peddlers or mobile repair services now, as there are so many.

3. The advisor starts visiting the home and begins a logbook to build up a written picture of the family and the present and/or proposed business.

4. When the business and the proposal are identified clearly, the advisor reports to the sub-office or the full team. The proposal can be anything from simple budgeting or book-keeping advice to substantial material or financial assistance.

5. If a loan or hire purchase assistance is requested, as is usually the case, then each advisor gets approval from the Programme Coordination. There is no set maximum loan, but bigger loans are considered more of a risk and problem.

6. A contract is drawn up (in front of a lawyer, if over £S1,000) with all the amounts and conditions. The whole process only takes a week now for short term loans and hire purchase. For "miniloans" of very small working capital to small groups of petty retailers, usually women, who act as guarantors for each other, it can be done in one day. These miniloans are charged at 1% a day, for up to one month.

7. The advisor follows up the case, monitors repayment and enters all details in the applicant's log book. More details are given later of the types of loans, but there are other important parts of the programme. There are the Industry Consultancy and Development Centres - they each house a sub-office and include "sheltered" workshop space, a marketing area, technical development workshops and a women's business area (each will hold about 40 businesses). There are also the Marketing and Supply Services - they look for supplies of tools, machinery and materials (eg sorghum to help the "injera" or pancake makers at a time of scarcity). They also seek bulk contracts and do sub-contracting, for instance, Oxfam ordered 5,000 children's dresses a month. A commission is charged by ACORD for these contracts obtained for the applicants.

Results/Evaluation
After the thirteen month investigation stage, the following objectives were set for the programme:

1) To promote welfare and development, by providing equal access to the means of producing wealth, resources for development and maximum participation in the development process.

2) To develop the economic strength of the informal sector and widen the range of commodities provided by it.

3) To enable clients to earn higher incomes.

4) To assist clients to create more employment opportunities.

5) To train and cultivate a cadre of local staff, who would be competent and determined enough to implement and ultimately to take over the programme.

The expatriate team, having set these objectives, began a very idiosyncratic process of forcing staff to take decisions, rather than pass them up the chain of command. The results at the end of 1985, after two years of operation, revealed a flexible and questioning service which certainly acheived its aims.

Client Numbers
    851 business clients (or client groups),
        196 of these had successfully completed the loan repayments and
            were continuing in their businesses.
        72 cases were closed as failures (only taking 4% of the loan fund).
        583 were ongoing.

There were also 91 home improvement loans, which had just started, for roofing materials and other items.

Client Statistics
    Hire purchase (loans up to 20 months) for tools and equipment:
        676 (35% Women), 517 still active, 112 completed, 47 failures.
    Short term loans (up to 2 months) for working capital:
        86 (44% Women), 32 still active, 49 completed, 5 failures.
    Hire purchase and short term loans combined:
        21 (48% Women), 9 still active, 8 completed, 4 failures.
    MicroCredit (up to one month):
        64 (44% Women), 25 still active, 23 completed, 16 failures.
    Consultancy Only (all clients received advice with loans):
        4 (50% Women).

Employment and Income

It is estimated, through the close monitoring of the logbooks, that the incomes of the clients had doubled from £S100 per month before the ACORD assistance. Of the 851 businesses that had been created, often there was more than one job in each and the assistance total was about 1,250 families.

Business Types (68% newly initiated, the rest existing businesses)

236 tailors	120 caterers	52 carpenters
140 water sellers	45 goods transporters	19 launderers
14 butchers	11 milk sellers	10 woven bed makers
10 cake makers	9 shoemakers	8 tyre repairers
6 goldsmiths	6 soft drink makers	6 reservoir operators
6 needle-workers	5 grinding mill operators	5 welders
5 painters	4 tinsmiths	4 pancake makers*
4 mattress makers	4 spaghetti makers	4 builders
4 electricity suppliers	4 perfume makers	3 radio repairers
3 bakers	3 hairdressers	3 fishermen
2 knitters	2 vegetable sellers	2 photographers
2 ice-cream makers	2"shiro"beanstew makers	1 mechanic
1 farmer	1 retailer	1 aluminium caster
1 pastry maker	1 tilly lamp maker	1 battery charger
1 singer	(* "injera")	

Updated Information

By the end of 1986, a full comparison was not available, but a further 226 businesses were helped: 75% were new businesses, and over the year there was a failure rate of approximately 15%. 25% were womens businesses and of the new businesses created about 60% were production based, 30% service and 10% retail.

Financial Details

The programme ran in 1985 at roughly US$750,000/year, of which a little more than one third went on local salaries, a third into the revolving loan and property development fund and the remainder was spent on staff development, training, the temporary expatriate personnel, logistic support, rents, and other costs. It now runs at about $600,000, with decreased capital input and expatriate staff. NOTE: the average official exchange rate of 2.45 £S per $, is used, but devaluation and inflation make this only a guide.

	£S
In 1985, the revolving fund statement was:	
End 1984 outstanding and 1985 new loans	691,880.54
Repayments of loans and hire purchase installments	353,438.44
End 1985 outstanding loans (incl. 29,124.29 Bad Debts)	338,442.10
Total Income (client charges, commission, rental and sales)	56,589.32
Expenditure (bad debts, Womens Centre purchases, expenses)	33,617.79
Net Income	22,917.53

(NOTE: Field Staff and Offices cost about £S17,000/month)

Using the 17 month period, from June 1984 to the end of 1985, the cost of assisting 851 businesses and 1,250 families is $1,062,500. These figures give a cost per business of $1,250 and a cost per job of $850. The figures show a high administration cost compared to the actual assistance given, but this level of examination and support to businesses is justified by the number of success stories.

In terms of income to the participants, if 1,250 people have increased their income by £S100 each month, this gives a total value of $612,245 per year. In other words the assistance has paid for itself within two years, and the businesses carry on bringing in income, without further assistance.

Comments

1. There has been constant experimentation with new strategies and structures - The programme is operating under very changeable conditions and has to adapt itself. In fact, the staff's salaries are tied to achievements, and positions rotate regularly to keep everybody in touch with the way their clients are responding.

2. This programme has actively avoided having preconceived set rules as to who it will help and how much it will lend. Instead it has tried to give the appropriate help, especially to the poorest and disadvantaged.

3. For pluralism - In such a mixed town community, the ACORD programme is seen to be fair and this is a strength to its work and to the staff. It is all too easy to help either the most powerful groups or particular groups and so be tainted by others with the charge of favouritism.

4. Decision-making and responsibility are favoured and indeed forced to the lowest level of the advisory staff. The operation of the programme depends on the decisions of the advisors, so they decide the policies and practices. Initially the staff found this difficult, as they could be blamed for any mistake, rather than passing the blame. But now this policy brings a competence and a flexibility, which can cope with the many problems presented. The reporting system is very thorough and open, to encourage discussion and comparison - and also praise and criticism.

5. Payment for services - Most Aid, particularly for refugees, is on a charitable basis. Here, not only is the loan repaid, but fees and administration costs are charged, though "interest" is not charged. This makes the loan acceptable to Islamic Law which allows fees and risk capital, but not interest as that is viewed as usury.

6. Only small businesses? - The first coordinators were single-minded in using a business approach to helping small businesses, and they produced a responsive and an efficient service. Certainly the best answers to problems in small businesses can be found within other small businesses and not in bureaucracies or other organizations. The coordinators would recognize that this programme is only one attack on poverty and there should be others, but they are critical of the "welfare" approach - it needs a business mind not a welfare mentality to help small businesses.

Yet Port Sudan and its refugees need many services. The home improvement loans mark ACORD's first step away from exclusively small business activities.

7. Only individuals? - Small business is essentially an individual affair; group activities need cooperation and clearly defined objectives - if these are not present, then you are just adding problems to an already difficult task. The miniloan groups were not forced, all the participants had to agree with the others about the joint repayment responsibility, even though businesses were independent of each other.

8. Careful preparation - This avoided false starts and therefore saved money, but the initial plan produced was not a blueprint to be followed; it was a starting point with initial directions. The difference between blueprint and evolving methods of planning projects is shown is section E.

9. The future of the programme - Although this programme goes further in self-financing than any other refugee IG programmes we studied, it is not clear whether such charges can eventually cover all the costs. The intention was for the programme to become a fully independent, non-profit agency, however outside grants continue to be necessary. So, at some point in the future, the programme may be taken over by government or other semi-official bodies, as a very cost-effective service to help the poor and to increase economic activity.

THE RELIEF END - Christian Outreach in East Sudan

Main Features

An expatriate volunteer administrator working for a medical programme saw a need combined with an opportunity: refugee weavers could make traditional cloth for refugee use. Between October 1985, when the local refugee commission agreed the proposal for this short-term relief substitution project, and the end of April 1986, when the Tigrean refugees moved on, the project produced cloth for the refugees and others.

Background

In one of the camps in East Sudan with a transit population of about 20,000, Christian Outreach set up a medical programme, from which an awareness developed of the refugees' other needs. The administrator (then aged twenty-two) first asked permission to do the weaving project, followed by a small agricultural training programme, together taking about a third of his time.

Programme Process

The programme aims were to provide an occupation, to increase incomes, to provide training and to provide suitable clothes for the refugees' return to Tigre, in that order. There were no other employment opportunities, except for very menial jobs, and the families wanted income immediately and also for their eventual return. It was also desirable to provide training for a few people, who were not skilled weavers and to make suitable, traditional clothes, which were more appropriate than those provided by donors. The "history of the problems", to use the administrators words, proceeded as follows:

1. Raw or Spun Cotton? - Since one of the scheme's objectives was to provide employment, and cotton spinning is very labour intensive, every effort was made to obtain raw cotton, rather than spun cotton. There was also a supply problem with the manufactured spun cotton. But the raw cotton chosen also had problems, it was dirty, off-white, and not of a good quality, though still possible to use. A whiter raw cotton was available, but only on the black market. Some spun cotton was bought later to diversify production.

2. Building the Looms - luckily some weavers were skilled at this.

3. The Weavers - Twelve people were employed - ten men, of whom two were TB patients, and two women. Their salaries were originally paid monthly, but were later changed, with some difficulty, to a piece-rate comparable to local weavers at about 0.3 US $/metre, giving about 50 $/month, which was still above other camp and local earnings.

4. The Spinners - These were all women, and indeed most women in the camp could spin. Their salaries started at 12 US $/kg after much discussion. After 60 kg had been made, the price was discovered to be high - a later contract price was 3 $/kg. But giving the cotton cloth in exchange for spinning was found to be even better - first at 12m then 6m cloth per kg spun cotton. This had the added advantage of distributing the cloth throughout the camp. Quality control was the supervisors' responsibility. With all the different systems of payment or exchange, the total number of women benefitting from the project was difficult to estimate - possibly 500.

5. Supervision - The expatriate administrator and the refugee supervisor kept records, checked production and carried out the marketing. The supervisor was originally on a monthly salary, but this was dropped in line with output, at the same time the weavers changed to piece-rate. This was mostly to prepare for a future hand-over, perhaps to being a cooperative, rather than for the sake of cost-cutting.

6. Distribution - By mid-April 1986, 4,167m of cloth had been produced, of which 2,579m was given in return for spinning, 698m was given to other refugees who did no work for the project. 216m was sold, and the remaining 674m stayed in stock or was used as samples for sales.

7. Marketing and the Future - At present production costs, the cotton cloth with the traditional coloured stripe ends can be produced at one US$/metre. The cost breakdown was:

> 11% cotton, 46% weaving, 38% spinning and
> 5% administration, supervisor, guard/watchman.

This is excluding expatriate costs, equipment or store costs, apart from the guard, but it does give the levels of costs should a cooperative be formed.

In the future, if the new refugees coming in can work in a similar project, then changes will be made in the marketing. There seem to be five possible directions:

- Local sales look possible, but difficult as there are local weavers and the people prefer white to off-white cloth.
- Three foreign agencies in Sudan have bought cloth for their programmes and could employ a couple of weavers full-time.
- Sales in the camp itself have started with a small commission (less than 5%), but while some cloth is distributed free this may be difficult.
- The cloth could be used to replace blankets, which cost $1.50 to transport to Sudan, if agencies would buy it.
- Or production could be sold to "Western Markets" in charity/3rd World shops.

All these possibilities need to be investigated further.

Results/Evaluation

As an example of relief substitution, this should be seen as only a beginning - it was production for and by refugees, but not direct substitution and could have gone further, such as producing blankets or substituting other clothes given to the refugees.

In terms of its objectives, the twelve weavers earned about $2,500 in six months and the estimated 500 spinners earned $4,300, not including the cloth exchanged for spinning. So perhaps the spinners were the main recipients of this programme. Training seems to have been a small part, though it might be bigger with the new refugees, in the future. Providing traditional cloth seems to have been an important aspect, though 2,579m must represent a small proportion of the need, in the context of the total refugee population of 20,000.

Financial Details

By the end of May 1986, the total costs were around $10,500, including about $1,000 for tools and equipment, but excluding the expatriate volunteer administrator. The remaining $9,500 for 4,167m is much higher than the $1/m given above, because for most months the higher rates were paid to the weavers, spinners and supervisor.

Comments

1. The main point is that where skills, supplies and needs coincide, then a scheme which fulfils many objectives can be started and be operational in a short time.

2. Even if the refugees return home quickly, this project proves that there are income-generating projects, which can support people, enhance or retain their skills, help others and be genuinely portable.

3. The progress of this project shows that it is difficult to "get it right" immediately. There are too many variables - and such starting problems cannot be used to evaluate the whole idea. This often means a costly starting period, which shows clearly in the overpayments to weavers and spinners, resulting in a cloth cost per metre of $2.28, instead of $1, which was the final production cost.

4. This agency collaborated with two other agencies to sell the cloth and another two in getting supplies. As in other IG projects, such cooperation is often essential.

5. In the final project evaluation by Christian Outreach, which proposed a continuation, it was stated ... "if the [new] project is to be a success ... [the administrator coming] does not need to know anything about weaving, although it would obviously help. What is needed is someone with ideas, energy, an eye for colours and patterns, and a business mind."

COMPARISONS BETWEEN THE CASE STUDIES

The following tables set out some comparisons between the five case studies. It would have been more informative to present these comparisons for all the programmes surveyed. However, these comparisons need a detailed understanding of each programme, and very few agencies record all of the statistics used below in enough detail. As it was, a number of "educated guesses" had to be made from figures or comments made by the case study respondents. As we said in the introduction, we have concentrated in this book on business programmes for refugees, so business starters and assistance schemes are more represented than other types of IG programme.

TABLE 1 - Income Generation Types, Training and Skills

Organization	IG activity types[a] (in descending order)	IG only?	Training/Advice[b] Given (0-5 scale)	Skill Levels of[c] Participants(0-5 scale)
AICF	6, 7	No	2	4
ARC	6,5,8,7	No	3	4
Quakers[d]	6,7,3,4	Mostly	3	3
ACORD	7	Yes	4	3/4
Chr.Outreach (CO)	1, 4	No	1	3

[a] = Activity types, 1=Relief Substitution, 2=Development investment, 3=Income Adding Starter
4=Basic Skill Utilization, 5=Vocational Training/Production, 6=Business Starters,
7=Business Assistance Scheme, 8=Employment Bureau.
[b] = Training/Advice scale, 1= None given, 2= Some given incidentally, 3= Part of project,
4= A main part of project, 5= Majority of project.
[c] = Skill Level Scale, 1= Unskilled, 2= a little experience, 3= Basic skill,
4= Some training, 5= Trained and qualified
[d] = Figures refer only to Loan/Advice Scheme, not other IG projects, except IG types.

Comments on Table 1 -

a) The first two columns support two of the conclusions from the questionnaire analysis - that although agency programmes are diverse, the types of IG projects can be classified into one or more of the eight types. Also only 30% of agencies run IG programmes exclusively.

b) The amount of training given seems to correspond to how far the refugees are from the relief phase. The further away, so the more training is given. This also correlates with moving away from relief to flexible development - the phases A. to E. in Figure 3. This is probably to be expected as training takes time to bear fruit, and is only practicable to organize, once the emergency phase is over.

c) Most of the participants in the programmes have had some training or experience. This means that neither the unskilled, nor the well-qualified are served by these programmes.

TABLE 2 - Timescales and Staffing Programme

	Programme Time-scale (years)	IG Time-scale (yrs)	Nos. Expats in IG (equivalent)	Nos. Local Staff in IG
AICF	5+	2+	0.5	6
ARC	6+	3+	0.5	20
Quakers[d]	4+	4+	0.7	3
ACORD	3+	3+	2	20
CO	2+	0.5	0.3	1

Comments on Table 2

a) Most programmes have been operating for rather longer than the IG projects within them. The questionnaire analysis also confirms this.

b) Nothing conclusive can be said about staffing levels, other than that the nature of the programme probably defines the number of expatriate and local staff.

TABLE 3 - Numbers and Costs

	Businesses/yr (Beneficiaries/yr)	Assistance. Cost in 1 yr $	Cost/Business /year [e,f] $	Expected Return in first yr [e,f] $	Ratio Assistance- to 1yr Return [e,f]
AICF	795 (1,129)	170,400[e]	214	609,660	1:3.6
ARC(ASAR)	916 (1,107)	250,000[e]	272	586,000	1:2.3
Quakers[d]	34 (85)[e]	12,000	350	13,200	1:1.1
ACORD	601 (882)[e]	750,000	1,250	367,000	1:0.49
CO	12 (2,000)[e]	12,500[e]	1,042	8,455	1:0.68

[e] = An Estimate made by the authors, from the information in the case studies.
[f] = See Evaluation Section Y.

Comments on Table 3

a) The numbers assisted in each project seem higher than equivalent projects with local people, but this may need more research to confirm.

b) More will be said about financial statistics in the Evaluation Section Y., but it is clear that the "payback" period, or more accurately the time taken for the income produced to equal the assistance cost is often less than a year. Alternatively, the "rate of return" for all except Christian Outreach, which did not continue, is over 50% - some bankers may envy this! And the majority of the refugees (about 80% on average) go on generating income with no further assistance!

c) Perhaps we should have included cost per job per year, as the cost per business per year does not include those businesses with many participants or extra jobs created, but we only had some figures. The Quakers helped 51 businesses, with 127 direct participants over 18 months. This gives a cost/job/yr of $142, comparable to the AICF figure of $151.

TABLE 4 - Issues of Coverage and Participation

	% IG to target population[g]	% Women	Activity Chosen by refugees	Assistance Chosen by refugees[h]	Cultural Understanding used (0-5 scale)[i]	Connections with other agencies (0-5 scale)[j]
AICF	0.2	4	Yes	No	4	2
ARC	0.05	34	Yes	No	5	5
Quakers[d]	0.7	40	Yes	Partly	4	4
ACORD	0.4[k]	40	Yes	Yes	4	3
CO	1.3	99	No	No	2	3

[g] = This is the percentage of IG recipients in the programme compared with the numbers of refugees in the area.

[h] = This really asks the question "does the refugee choose the type of assistance given to him or her?"

[i] = Cultural Understanding Scale, 1= No attempt to adapt programme to culture, 2= Some changes made during the project, 3= Some adaptions made to fit project to the culture before and during the project, 4= Cultural considerations an integral part of project design and operation, 5= As 4, but including helping other agencies to plan for these factors.

[j] = Other agencies Connections Scale, 1= No connections, 2= A few connections, 3= Some programme connections, 4= Other agencies are involved in a part of the programme, 5= As well as 4, agency also acts in a coordination role for other agencies.

[k] = Only refers to refugee clients from refugee population in Port Sudan.

Comments on Table 4 -

a) It is worth noting that most of these programmes deal with less than one per cent of the refugee population. That would seem to suggest that more programmes of this type are needed, since there are almost certainly far larger numbers of refugees with the necessary skills and experience than those assisted. It also suggests that more programmes are needed for those less skilled, when a comparison is made with Table 1.

b) The columns showing whether the activities and the assistance given were chosen by the refugees, show agreement with our theory of more "developmental style" in the move from relief to flexible development. Christian Outreach is near the relief style, ARC and AICF are the next nearest, with the Quakers and then ACORD being nearer a developmental style. The amount of choice of activity or assistance also follows the same progression towards the increased participation of the refugees.

This admittedly subjective assessment of these last two columns show that in the field of IG at least, agencies are aware of the importance of cultural backround and of the need to cooperate with others.

THREE REFUGEE BUSINESSES (See Photographs on P.46)

Having given five case studies of agencies' programmes, it is now time to look at businesses from the refugees' points of view. Below are three short sketches of real refugees whose businesses have been assisted by agencies. There follow two imaginary "average" refugees, whose history and businesses are the averages of all the questionnaire data of the men or women in those countries. See also section R. - "The Refugees' Viewpoint" for more information from the refugee business questionnaires.

1. Hassan the Stone-cutter

In June 1984, Hassan was one of six members of a stone-cutting group that received a loan from the Quakers in the Daray Macaane Refugee Camp in Somalia. The loan was for 6,870 Somali Shillings, then equivalent to $430, to buy hammers, chisels, crowbars and other tools. During the first three months the group managed to get contracts to sell their cut stone to builders in the local town of Boroma. However, building houses needs water for the cement or mud binding and this was the beginning of the 1984/5 drought. For the next five months, until two rainy days in March (instead of the usual twenty), Hassan and the group went on cutting stones, but sold none. They built up small mounds of cut stones on the hillsides instead.

The Quakers agreed to reschedule the loan - only taking repayments on the months the group sold stones. When the normal rains came at the end of September 1985, they had paid back 5 out of 15 possible monthly repayments. They had worked for nothing for most of that time, but the stocks meant that they were able to finish repayments by March 1986. See the Quaker Business Analysis Form in section U. for the stone-cutters original plans.

2. Abdida the Tailor

Abdida came from Afghanistan early in 1984, and was living in a very old tent with many holes when the Austrian Relief Committee found her in a refugee village in Pakistan. She was given a sewing machine and by September 1985, on a return monitoring visit, ARC found that she had earned enough money to pay for the building of a comparatively large mud house. Not only that, but she had bought a tailoring table with a machine cover. She was the first woman that ARC had seen reinvesting in her business.

(In the photograph, the rule of Purdah is observed and her face is covered).

3. Mohammed the Dressmaker

In the photograph Mohammed (on the right) is explaining his secret pleating process to Hussein, a Partnership for Productivity Business Advisor in Somalia. He folds the cloth on a cardboard frame and then it is steamed above an ordinary Somali charcoal cooker in the pipe behind them. Mohammed is a self-settled refugee in Hargeisa, the second biggest town in Somalia, and his business is thriving. Hussein taught Mohammed how to prepare simple accounts, so that Mohammed could easily see which items made him the most money. Hussein was then able to introduce Mohammed to some clothing retailers, to improve Mohammed's market and enable him to spend more time pressing pleats and less time trying to sell his dresses.

1. Hassan the Stone-cutter   2. Mohammed the Dress-maker

3. Abdida the Tailor

TWO TYPICAL REFUGEES - A WOMAN AND A MAN.

Having given three cases of real refugees - two men in Somalia and one woman in Pakistan, we wanted to give more typical examples of an average man and woman, in and from rural areas. We have chosen a woman in Sudan and a man in Pakistan. "Amina" is the average of fourteen women in Sudan and "Ahmed" is the average of twenty-eight men in Pakistan. Both represent the average of all the examples of that type we received in our refugee business questionnaires from the agencies, so they may not be entirely typical. The averages of all the refugee business questionnaires are in appendix C.

Both Ahmed and Amina have final profits rather higher than the average refugees' income in those countries, but they do give a general impression of the average situation for those refugees in business.

AMINA IN SUDAN

Amina is 33 years old and has been a refugee for five years, but has only been receiving free rations for three years. She has two adults and three children who depend on her income. Her parents owned a teashop in Ethiopia and that is what she started in Sudan. She received $180 loan from a agency Business Starter scheme. Her business has a turnover of $170 each month, her income is $70 and she also pays back $10 of the loan. She values the visits of the business advisor, as each time he suggests something new, which brings in new customers. Last month, it was a sign at the end of the street, because her business is not on a main road. One of her daughters works for her when the school is closed and a cousin works at lunch-times only.

When Amina started her biggest problems were getting money to start, and then getting customers. Now she is thinking about moving to bigger premises with more people around. Sometimes she gets sick from cooking over a smoky fire, so she hopes that she can do less cooking after the move. She feels she is settled and is not thinking about returning, but wishes the troubles would end so she can go home.

AHMED IN PAKISTAN

Ahmed is 33 and has also been a refugee for five years, but has only had free rations for one year, as he works as a blacksmith in the local town. He has three adult and four child dependents. He brought a few tools with him and had saved $80 from working for someone else. Two years ago an agency added $200 worth of equipment as a grant and now his turnover is $140 each month. From this he takes home $60 each month. His eldest son helps his father and is learning the trade. Ahmed employs another refugee from the same valley in Afghanistan where he grew up and where he used to work as a blacksmith.

Before the agency grant, Ahmed's main problems were getting enough capital to start and finding cheap scrap metal supplies. He is now thinking about learning better welding, which is a course offered by another agency. He thanks Pakistan for giving him a home and although he cannot own land, housing or fixed machinery, he thinks this is fair - anyway he wants to return to Afghanistan when the situation changes. There seems to be more competition now as other businesses are starting, and Ahmed wants a loan for a small welding machine so he can expand into a business with fewer competitors.

FACTORS FOR CONSIDERATION - Before Starting

A. FOR ALL AGENCIES

A1. Introduction

In keeping with our intention to make this a reference book for those interested in income-generating projects with refugees, we have divided up the topics, so that each section is easy to find. However, as with any complex subject, some topics overlap many sections. So, rather than duplicate these in each section, we would hope the reader will go through it all once and then return to the parts useful to him or her. One obvious example of this is Evaluation, which should be dealt with at the beginning, during the running and at the end of any project. We have placed it at the end (under section Y), in common with usual practice, but we would see Evaluation as more important than its position in the text suggests.

Given the wide diversity of agency, political, social and environmental contexts field workers must work with, there is little point in us providing a recipe for action. However we would like in the following pages to illustrate the range of possibilities and options which may be open to those embarking on an income-generating programme. Wherever possible we will give examples from our research of agencies' experiences in specific situations.

We would recommend a degree of wariness in using this material, in that each refugee situation is different. There are different skills and cultures, different political situations, different environments and different agencies. The reader should pick and choose what is relevant. So, our theme is "Be wary of answers"; we will try to give the questions that arose from the research and the answers given. We do give our opinions, but it is up to the reader to judge from the evidence for their own particular situation.

A2. What are the most important factors for success with IG projects?

Responses to the qualitative questionnaire B suggested that the participation of the refugees, the opportunities allowed by the host government and the refugees' skills are the most important factors, in that order. From the other factors identified by the respondents, a good knowledge of the cultural backround of both the refugees and local peoples is also essential. Whereas the educational levels and the low capital available to refugees seem relatively unimportant.

More details on these are given later, but to interpret these comments and so to design and run I.G. projects, we have suggested that an understanding of the time-scale of the refugees' perceptions of their stay within the host country's political situation is also very important. That is why the "Framework for Thinking" about the types and timing of income generating projects is at the beginning of this manual and not in this section.

The importance of the host country situation and the time-scale is corroborated by many respondents. In Question B9., "The Opportunities allowed by Government", is seen as even more important than the skills of the refugees. In fact the failure to understand the host country situation is seen as one of the main factors that leads to the failure of I.G. projects (Q.B24). And the time-scale factor ranks just after the refugees' cultural backround in importance (Q.B6 and 23).

A3. Refugee Participation and Initiation in IG projects

Participation is identified as the most important factor, but its meaning is vague. Refugees can "participate" by merely being assisted or can participate by running and controlling the programme. Certainly our respondents felt that those projects or businesses initiated by refugees should be supported and that they work better than outside initiatives. However, most I.G. projects are initiated from outside, which suggests more factors are involved when agencies decide to initiate projects themselves. Some agencies see the refugees as having limited flexibility or unfocussed enthusiasm or as suffering from dependancy symptoms, arising from their new position as refugees.

Certainly, real and psychological dependency exists at the relief phase, but they cannot be said to be permanent. We suggested earlier that the trend from relief to flexible development should be accompanied by similar trends from dependence to independence and from employment to self-employment. There must be the same trend for refugee participation and initiation. The current situation for relief substitution projects is one where the projects are initiated by the agency, the products and the participants are chosen by the agency and the organization controlled by the agency. By the time refugees enter the phase for business assistance projects the situation has changed. The business, the assistance and the organization, at least of their own business, is controlled by the refugee, only the project is still agency-initiated and run. Four of our respondents described this process as a "developmental" style - which is also more participatory.

A4. What does "Cultural Background" mean?

Although the understanding of the economic/cultural and political background of the refugees and the host population was given one of the highest values in the replies, its meaning is again vague. Obviously, it means responding to the particular situation, but an agency field worker cannot think of everything, so what are common elements? The following list is not all-inclusive and in different situations one might be very much more important than another:

- Balances between groups - there are very often sub-groups of refugees, which vary in their power and wealth. A careful understanding of this can avoid bitter disputes. Such careful balances were features of the AICF and ARC case studies.

- Balances between the sexes - more is written of this later. But, for instance, if all the staff are men or the assistance only provided for full-time businesses, then the number of women is likely to be low.

- Religious concerns - the Islamic concept of a loan is an obvious one (see p.38).

- Legal concerns - the ownership of apparently unused land has caused tremendous problems to refugees and local people, especially farmers.

- Ecological concerns - starting many lime or charcoal-making businesses puts a strain on the wood resources of an area.

- Wage levels - one common dispute occurs when an agency comes in and pays more than normal for the area, and so causes dissention throughout the refugee and local populations. (See the Christian Outreach Case study).

- Loan or Grant levels - there is a skill in getting them at the right levels. Too low and businesses fail, too high and the queue shows it is more important to get the assistance, than to run a business.

A last point is that - refugees may not distinguish between the different agencies who question them in order to "get to know them better." This has led to some refugees being annoyed at being asked the same questions again and still not getting any benefits. Also the same questioning has led to whisperings of "spies", which is not surprising from people who have just fled one country for another. Some questions may be particularly sensitive and it may not be possible to ask them directly.

A5. Project Type and Finance

It is complicated to get comparable figures from agencies, for many reasons - they may have aggregate figures for a number of projects or the categories were not defined in the same way or one particular figure needed was missing. So the following table is only a guide:

TABLE 5 - IG Project Types and Costs

IG TYPE	No. of organizations (% of 149 projects)	No. of participants direct (indirect)	Total cost ($/Yr)	Average cost ($) direct (indirect) participants
Relief substitution	2 (5)	4,510 (112,610)	1,828,000	405 (16)
Development investment				
* Infrastructure	1 (3)	2,018	5,540,000	2,745
* Environment	1 (3)	76 (20,000)	350,000	4,605(17.5)
Income-adding starters	2 (17)	340	29.000	85
Basic skill utilization				
* Agriculture	0 (9)	-	-	-
* Village crafts	2 (9)	5,300	36,500	7
Vocational training	(26)*			
* Skilled crafts	2	890	1,580,000	1,775
* Simple Vocational	2	400	10,000	25
Business starters	3 (22)	1,817	459,000	253
Business assistance	3 (6)	945	851,000	901
Employment bureau	1 (1)	120	15,000	125
	19(100%)			

(* Percentage not separable)

These results represent 19 organizations, for which we have details; with one column showing the percentages of the different IG types for the 149 organizations in the total survey. The participants can be either employed or self-employed, no split was possible. But what do they mean?

In Relief Substitution Projects, the main beneficiaries are the refugees that receive the quilts, school bags or school uniforms. The workers' wages make up only a quarter of the total assistance cost.

For Development Investment, the Infrastructure project was to create irrigation canals, but no numbers were given for those who would finally benefit, so it is difficult to analyse. The Environment project was set up to make fuel-efficient stoves and ovens and the main beneficiaries were the recipients of these (see case study on P.75).

As already discussed, agriculture projects are not generally included. The other skills that many refugees bring are handicraft skills. These handicrafts are sold to local and to foreign markets, so most of the costs are recovered and the low figures relate mostly to initial start-up costs.

It is clear from the above table that as the assistance moves from what we have called income-adding starters through business starters to business assistance, the cost per participant goes from $85 to $253 and then to $901. Gradually the average capital costs of helping each refugee increases as each "business" becomes more complex.

It is important to remember that most of this assistance is in the form of loans, and loan amounts have been included in the costs. As over 90% of the loans are repaid, the costs quoted above are substantially overstated.

This process of costs increasing with complexity is mirrored by the results from the Refugee Business Questionnaire. The results show that urban refugees in relatively developed areas, such as Nairobi in Kenya and towns on the West Bank average $3,900 per business, whereas the starting costs for rural refugees in Pakistan, Somalia and Sudan average $197 each.

The costs of Vocational Training varied so widely, we made two categories, one for skilled trades like automobile engineering and one for simple trades, like weaving, which can be done without infrastructural support or imported machinery. The differences speak for themselves.

We only have one case of an Employment Bureau - it was set up by the Austrian Relief Committee in Pakistan, which later closed - see ARC case study and section O. for further details on employment bureaux.

A6. How large should an IG project be?

As there are large numbers of refugees in poor countries, one of the aims of income-generating projects is to assist as many refugees as possible. But equivalent enterprise assistance projects working with nationals in poor countries have generally been found to be more effective when they are themselves small scale and acting in a local context. Most refugee projects are, however, operating on a far larger scale.

On average, each of the projects in our survey dealt with 842 people over the last twelve months, and three-quarters of them are acting in more than one site; the average is eighteen sites each.

Does this mean that all refugee IG projects must be large? No, even in countries with very large refugee populations, there are succesful projects with small numbers.

Is a loss of quality associated with this difference of larger projects for refugees? Generally, these large refugee projects are well-targeted and successful, but there is some evidence that loan repayments are reduced if the scheme is not in regular, direct contact with its participants. The success of ARC and AICF in giving tool kits to help start large numbers of refugee businesses, without regular contact, did show one way how large well-targeted projects can work.

Many of our respondents did favour local area bases. Even if they dealt with large numbers, they preferred a number of separate bases well coordinated, but relatively independent. ACORD had six such bases in the poorer districts of Port Sudan, as described in the case study.

Another approach was to start on a small or an experimental basis and gradually to grow in size. Some respondents felt that increasing the size of projects, increases the problems of communications and transportation and decreases opportunities for participation. They were sure that national programmes were less likely to be a success than regional ones, for these reasons.

One respondent wondered whether voluntary agencies or non-governmental organizations are inherently unsuited to run large projects, as their own internal organizations are small scale. Another respondent wondered whether governments or large international agencies could be flexible and responsive enough for IG projects. Size is not considered to be a major factor: both large and small projects can be good or bad, and the key is the sensitivity of the agency to the refugees situation.

The size of the project must fit the conditions - the refugees skills, the market and the local situation. Clearly there have been cases where too many people have been trained in skills that have no market, or too many businesses started which were dependent on one scarce resource material: large scale can be a problem, not only from an organizational point of view. Having said that, perhaps particularly with refugee projects, it is obviously necessary to help as many people as possible and this may mean looking more closely at cost-effectiveness than is done at the moment. There is a danger, as one respondent said, that charities feel they are automatically doing good when they give aid, whereas the truth according to another respondent is "give grants, you assist them [the refugees] to death."

A7. Expatriate and Local Staff

Although the following figures need some care in interpretation, it appears that the agencies which replied to our questionnaires have on average two and a half expatriate staff each, of whom two are working on IG. They are on average assisted by 70 local staff. If we exclude the big relief substitution, infrastructure and village craft projects, we come down to two expatriate staff with one working on IG, supported by 15 local staff. Given that for most agencies IG is only one part of their programme, this indicates that IG takes a lot of staff time. That is certainly the case in the IG projects the authors have known.

The costs of expatriate salaries compared to the total assistance given were not in the questionnaire, but from the case studies and other programmes with the information available in detail, it seems consistent at about 16%. It is possible to reduce this figure with competent local staff, whether they be refugees or nationals of the host country. Programmes with high expatriate salaries, such as are paid by some American or international aid agencies, need to justify these in terms of numbers assisted, as this causes resentment from both host nationals and refugees. Even the relatively cheap expatriate volunteers must be careful not to be helping just a few people.

The difficulty of obtaining competent local staff seems to be only an issue in the poorest areas of Somalia and Sudan, where on-the-job training and internal courses for staff are normal. In Kenya and Pakistan, more staff are already trained, although some on-the-job training continues. The skill of the staff is one of the main factors mentioned in the "Any other lessons learned" section of the questionnaire; the success of IG projects is said to depend very much on the good choice and use of local staff. Although the respondents gave few clues on how to choose staff, they did give some questions about local staff when projects are being planned, which are shown in section E.11. Later, in section Q., we look at choosing the participants, which obviously also affects the choice of staff.

B. FOR RELIEF AGENCIES THINKING ABOUT DEVELOPMENT

B1. The nature of Relief Agencies

Relief Agencies should be good at moving relief assistance in quickly and efficiently, which means they have a number of characteristics:

Time-scale - they work to a short time-scale, in fact most personnel in this period are on 6 months or shorter contracts. Their supplies must be ready within weeks, since any day lost could mean lives lost as well.

Organization - logistics and statistics: they need to be skilled in these fields and able to decide quickly how much is needed for how many and when. The agency must be prepared with its own systems already set up, in order to answer these questions.

Resources - food, water and health resources have to be provided quickly, and given the usual lack (or perceived lack) of local resources, that means that they come in from outside.

B2. Are Relief Agencies suited to promote Income-Generation?

Despite several comments from the questionnaire respondents along the lines that "IG needs a business-type mentality", the answer has to be "Yes". Only 30% of agencies are involved in IG programmes alone, and three out of the five programmes described in the case studies started and remain mainly Health programmes.

In fact, being already with the refugees has two main advantages. Firstly, the refugees know and hopefully trust and understand the agency, which gives the agency credibility to start something new. Secondly, working on any project, perhaps particularly health projects, the agency builds up knowledge of the refugees' skills, organization, their cultural backround and their expressed needs, as well as their objective needs.

Besides these two there are other advantages, which may apply in some situations. The host government organization already knows the agency and its personnel, which may give that agency an advantage over newly arrived agencies. If getting registered as a legal entity in the host country is a slow process, it can save time and money, especially for outside donors, to adapt the work of an existing agency than bring in a new one.

B3. What changes need to be made for a Relief Agency to run IG projects?

Most of the changes needed involve changing from a relief style agency to a development style one (See section C.1). But what particular changes are needed?

Funding and Staff Contracts - Staff should have longer contracts, funding should be assured over longer periods.

Use local resources and local people - The programmes should use local resources and local people, for instance trainers should be local small businessmen or women, whenever possible.

Use refugees - Programmes should try not to import goods, but should use their agency buying power to get items made locally or preferably by the refugees. Of 17 IG programmes, only 7 bought from refugees:

2 handicraft or relief substitution ones obviously buy from the refugees.
2 other projects buy some refugee production.
3 buy a little, like charcoal or pots from businesses that make them.

We feel that the use of the agencies' buying power could be increased, so that much of the refugees' and agencies' needs could be supplied by the refugees. However some agencies make this difficult by international tendering restrictions - one soap-making project could not compete with free imported soap! The money so entering the refugee economy, can then help other businesses start to supply the refugees' needs.

Attitude and Style Changes - These are the biggest changes; refugees must be helped to do things for themselves. The starving, helpless refugee image must give way to the independant, proud refugee, who has overcome the difficulties. Most people have heard of the old chinese proverb "Give a man a fish, you feed him for one day, teach a man to fish you feed him for life". Many development agencies have gone one further; they have helped people to decide what they want to do, and what they want to learn and then to take control over their own destinies. When pollution or fishing quotas stop the fishing, then he or she can plan and decide what to do and yet another assistance project is not needed.

The management style of the project has to change. What started as relief for the starving must move towards flexible development of people who are in charge of their own lives. The refugees were starving, they are poor, they need assistance, but not charity. We hope that the change will be gradual and progressive. The agency must try to aim to "put itself out of business", rather than to continue running the project.

We cannot claim that such a process will be smooth or can be completed, but it does seem to match the major trends in several countries with refugees awaiting one of the durable solutions (see p.4 and p.8).

Dependency - This is a complex topic, but as one respondent said, "it is a visible factor". About half the respondents felt that dependency arose from the loss of the refugees' former lives, the other half felt that much of it came from the relief process itself, where everything is done for them. A few respondents likened refugees to people who are colonized, and who wait for things to happen to them. Whatever its reasons, everybody felt dependency is an important problem, and can cause depression and inertia.

Workers in income-generating projects need to be aware and actively plan to avoid dependency. The main ways of doing this included "having a built-in withdrawal", a "self-sustaining aspect" and involving refugees "in the decisions and self-help of camp life".

C. FOR DEVELOPMENT AGENCIES THINKING ABOUT REFUGEES

C1. The nature of Development Agencies

Agencies which are involved in "ordinary" development, among people who are not refugees, have a number of characteristics which enable them to try to help the people in an area improve their situation:

Time-scale - they work on as long a period as they can rely on funding, employing staff for two years or more and making programme plans for longer.

Organization - people and participation; the agency must ask itself who is doing what, why and how? The agency must be prepared to negotiate and to compromise, to learn from its failures and to experiment with new directions.

Resources - if the people who are being assisted, are to continue on their own, they must rely on local resources or local organizations and the development agency must therefore work to make itself redundant from the very beginning.

C2. What changes need to be made for a Development Agency to work with refugees?

Income-generating projects are, by nature, developmental and longer term than relief projects. But what are the differences between working with refugees and working on very similar projects with local people in developing countries? Two have already been touched upon - time-scale and psychological factors, but these will be repeated and extended here:

Time-scale - Within a few months of the emergency, the first businesses appear (usually without assistance). These and the first assisted projects or businesses encourage others to start something. However, unlike similar local business people, the refugees are more likely to prefer taking a chance and looking at opportunities in days and months, rather than years.
  One respondent wrote - "The future is so uncertain that it is todays meal that is most important - an appropriate enterprise for the present". As the years pass, so the time-scale that refugees contemplate extends, but it is a matter of careful judgement as to what time-scale a particular group of refugees is thinking about at a particular time. For instance, the first training courses may only last weeks or months, but later one whole year may be acceptable.

Psychology - Although definitely not schizophrenic, the refugees attitude is at the same time both more radical and more conservative, than that of local people. This is both useful and detrimental to income-generating endeavours. The agency must somehow tap the "community adrenaline", that is its willingness to take on new ideas, without suffering from the "bandwagon effect" which may lead, for example, to six tailors asking for a loan the morning after one tailor's loan was approved.
  Often an agency can use the refugee elders to combine the conservative and radical positions; the elders can play a leading role in beginning new ideas, while maintaining their traditional respect. However, an unintended slight to the elders, can stop any proposal completely, showing the negative side of these psychological attitudes.

"Portability" - If return or resettlement are more likely than integration, even if only in the refugees' minds, then any assistance given should take account of the need to be "portable". By this we mean that perhaps buildings should not be permanent, training should only be given in skills that can also be carried out in the countries that the refugees are likely to go to, and machinery and tools which are provided should actually be physically portable. The nature of "portability" depends on the enterprise and the type of assistance: not everything can be portable, offices, training schools and irrigation canals cannot be moved easily!

Whereas most development projects aim to make things long-lasting and durable, that might not be the right direction for refugee projects. There may be other reasons for more durability; for instance, new workshops could eventually become assets for the host government and people. New water sources could also help the local population as well as the refugees.

Working with groups - Many development agencies prefer to work with groups of local people on a common long-term interest, rather than with individuals. However, most respondents felt that individual refugees are more likely to succeed than groups. The reasons for this included - the independent nature of many refugees (and within their culture), the need for speed in starting projects and to avaoid disputes in the organization of the enterprise.

A similar debate arises with co-operatives - is the value of working together negated by its difficulties? Our respondents did not answer this, but did suggest that as a first thought projects should assist individuals (and their families). This is not to say avoid all groups: some activities can only be done as groups, such as mass quilt making and others, suc as those sharing group credit responsibility can be successful. There is one more proviso - women seem to work better in groups than men.

However, it does seem that development agencies should adjust to thinking about individuals, rather than groups of refugees. Perhaps this shows another psychological aspect of refugees - they are thinking more closely about their families and the present, rather than the wider community and the future, which are the building blocks of group action.

D. PROGRAMME OBJECTIVES

D1. Introduction

Specific programme objectives must depend very much on the political, environmental, business and social context in which the agency is working, and the agency's and the field workers' own ideology and style of working. The funding agencies and the host government departments responsible for refugees or particular activities, such as commerce, must also be considered. AND there are the refugees' needs and wants. It looks very complex. Can it be simplified?

In discussion of objectives, it is important to distinguish clearly between the following three rather different things, which are often confused with one another:

> Programme (or agency) Goals - those statements which set the direction for the programme or projects. Such statements as "To assist the refugees with income-generating projects" or "To help the refugees become self-supporting" or "To improve the quality of life for the refugees". These cannot be evaluated easily, nor should they be, as they are putting forward a hope, rather than stating a definite intention.

> Programme Objectives - These are statements of general intention, which can be measured or inferred from measurements. These objectives should not be anything that can be quantified, they must relate to the goals. For instance, a village handicraft scheme, with a goal of helping the refugees to become self-supporting, should have an objective of creating 100 businesses, that are operating and independent. Such an objective can be inferred from measurements of loan repayment or by visits. That scheme should not have the objective to have given 100 looms to the refugees, with no broader aim in mind.
>
> Some objectives can be difficult to measure directly, such as the profit taken in a business, but can be inferred from "indicators".

> Objective or Goal Indicators - Indicators are very specific measurable changes that support the objective or goal statement. For a goal such as to improve the quality of life, indicators like reduced child mortality or the numbers and variety of shops in the market can show the goal is being reached. For an objective "to give the refugees income" can be indicated by regular loan repayments or by the numbers of businesses still operating six months after having received a tool-kit.

Despite what appears to be general agreement on the importance of thinking through objectives, in practice the value of objectives varies, depending on their relevance to what actually happens in programme implementation. It is important not to be bound entirely by objectives which were probably formulated elsewhere: even the goals which appeared most urgent, may have to give place to others, once close personal contact has revealed more of the situation

D2. Objectives in Practice

Of the 23 agencies that replied with a completed questionnaire, only 10 filled in Q.A30 on objectives, goals and aims, which probably says something in itself. Their answers, with the numbers of agencies saying each given in brackets, are summarised below:

> To give refugees income (3)
> To stimulate the growth (2) and stability (1) of small enterprises.
> To give employment - to as many as possible (2)
> To assist skilled refugees (2)
> To train for the future (2)
> To keep the refugees healthy and improve their quality of life (2)
> To become self-supporting (1)
> To introduce new, fuel-saving, equipment (1)

D3. Why Improve Objectives?

In most cases there is a gap between objectives in theory and in practice. Sometimes the goals are inherent in the agencies' style of working, so never get written down. Sometimes it is not completely clear what needs to be done, so even the basic objectives need to evolve as work progresses. Sometimes people design projects to evolve and do not want to commit themselves to fixed objectives. There are many other reasons, but we feel it is important to spend more time on the objectives at the beginning of a project for three reasons:

1. It helps the staff, head office and others, such as funding agencies, to be clear on what the programme or project is to do. It has been known for agencies to have been evaluated on what they should have done, because the objectives were vague or non-existent and such a process nearly always involves recriminations.

2. If conditions change, in one or more parts of the programme, as they nearly always do, then field staff can refer back to the original objectives for new directions, or consult back to head office for changed objectives.

3. During the programme, new facts or opportunities emerge. If the objectives are clear, then these can be acted on or neglected, so that the programme does not change into something else, without careful thought.

D4. What should the Objectives be?

What objectives should refugee IG programmes or projects have? It is very difficult to generalize, but here are some points that came out of the reports and questionnaires:

a) The objectives should say how many refugees, the methods to be used, where it is to be done and for how long. Often the estimated number of indirect beneficiaries should be included for example, families, or those receiving relief substitution items.

b) It is of the essence of most income-generating assistance projects that refugees should be self-sufficient, or at least have some continuing source of income, when the project withdraws or before. The objectives must cover this, by stating what the refugees are expected to be doing at the end of the project period. This might include the number of independant businesses, the percentage increase in family income or the number who have found jobs. Such objectives should take account of a realistic failure rate, for example on the number of loans successfully repaid.

c) The wording of the objectives should be sufficiently general to allow for change and evolution, but sufficiently specific to give an understanding of what the programme or project is planned to do. This is not easy, but is worth a great deal of effort.

d) Where there are social goals or objectives, such as "training for the future" or "improve the quality of life" or "to assist the formation of an appropriate organization to continue the work", then some form of indicator, should be written into the objective. It cannot be stressed too often that inputs such as training courses, equipment, buildings or institutions are means rather than ends; they should be treated as "investments", or "costs", and the objectives should include the "returns" or the "profits" that are expected to result from these inputs.

e) In development projects, one of the main goals is the self-sustainability of the activities, which can be indicated by the disappearance of the agency or the need for it. However, refugees in the flexible development phase, are in a special limbo, with one or more constraints on such a goal. It may be that such self-sufficiency objectives need to have limits; for some refugees this may mean not giving up the receipt of free rations, should they become economically self-sufficient, just in case of future changes. Each different constraint on self-sufficiency needs a deep understanding of the situation.

D4. Other Sections covering aspects of Objectives.

More details of objectives suitable for the eight different types of IG projects are shown in those sections dealing with each type - see sections H. to O.
    The sections X. and Y. respectively, on "Ending the Project" and "Evaluation", also deal with aspects of Objectives.

E. PLANNING PROJECTS

E1. Introduction

Project planning takes place at the same time as the objectives are being set. Even if the agency has decided on a specific IG project, there seem to be four different approaches to the way it can be planned: "informal", "learning by doing","formal" and "pre-planned".

The informal process gradually builds up a knowledge of the area and the people before making decisions, preferably with the people involved. The "learning by doing" approach starts by trying out directions, sometimes using very small-scale experimental projects and thus evolving broader directions for what is to be done. The formal process is often called something like a Feasibility Study or a Pilot Project and is normal when an agency has previously committed itself to some particular, if not defined course of action. The preplanned process, involves taking other projects and replicating some or all of their characteristics in a new project. It is important to decide which planning process will be used, before determining which questions need to be answered.

E2. The Informal Approach

Agencies or field workers using the informal approach build up their knowledge and understanding of the social and political environment and peoples' real needs in rather an informal way. This approach is often followed by community development workers or people in religious organizations, who have time to build up credibility in the area.

Also, people working with agencies already involved with other activities, like Health and Education, as already mentioned, can follow the informal approach in parallel with their existing activities, before launching an IG programme. By adopting this approach, it may be possible to avoid those mistakes which come from not understanding the cultural background - so saving money and time and effort. Making time to get to know local administrations, local people and refugees can pay dividends in the long term.

Understanding the local situation, was the most mentioned "Other factor for success" in our qualitative survey and was stressed by the Quakers and by ACORD. The second most important lesson was the corrolary of this that "Speed = Failure". Nevertheless the reality is often rather different; many workers do not have the luxury of time on their side - head offices (and more indirectly funding agencies) expect tangible results sooner rather than later.

Host governments also too often expect an agency to offer tangible material assistance as soon as possible, particularly after the relief phase. And, not least the refugees themselves have high expectations of speedy material help - they do not appreciate foreigners, who seem to them to be sitting around doing very little. The refugees may have been asked many times before what they need and are frustrated by hearing nothing further.

For these reasons, a purely informal approach is unlikely to work in refugee settings. We did come across one example of an agency leaving partly because they used the informal approach. This was during the relief phase, when neither the refugees nor the host government understood why the material help was not immediately forthcoming.

E3. Learning by Doing

Learning by small-scale experiments, rather than by merely having discussions can, if successful, overcome the immediate problems of suspicion and raised expectations, which the field worker may meet. It may also be a very effective way for the workers to learn more about the real problems of the refugees.

It is good public relations to be seen, both by the authorities and the refugees, to be getting down to work quickly. Some information may be readily available - from the agency's own prior research, other agencies' research, some preliminary meetings with the administrations and the refugee leaders, and not least common sense! For instance, it seems that White Leghorn chickens are given to refugees the world over and they keep dying - the poor birds are bred for battery conditions and unless they have good owners, they die from disease or poor food. A little thought in talking to agencies and to local chicken farmers might help. Or a very small-scale pilot scheme could be started from which new breeds or rearing practices could be tried and improved, taking into account local modifications.

It is a lot easier to ask questions and elicit answers when actually trying to assist people, as opposed to carrying out a survey. The big danger, of course, is early failure through a lack of understanding of the situation. It may also be difficult to change paths that appear to have been set; for example switching from grants to loans or from loans to business advice in a business asssistance programme.

In spite of its advantages, learning by doing is rather unusual, partly because funding agencies do not often give money for experimentation, partly because host governments are impressed by large projects and perhaps because on all sides it looks as though the agency does not know what it is doing if it has to start with experiments.

E4. The Formal Approach

There is a basic distinction between the formal approach and those mentioned above. Some agencies like to identify as much as possible with the refugees through learning about their life-styles and customs, while others attach more importance to more formal and objective methods, such as comprehensive feasibility or market surveys.

Such studies can provide field workers with much useful statistical information about the lifestyles and needs of refugees for possible use in the future. Often, however, the information can be too general to be of specific assistance in designing a programme. The process itself can cause problems with refugees who are wary of outsiders or by raising their expectations. For instance, doing a full market survey on all the shoemakers in a camp - their skills, difficulties, the type of assistance they require, the market potential, and other information, may only serve to give the field worker many pages of figures and writing, and may cause many angry shoemakers to come banging on the door, their expectations raised but unable to be met by the agency!

Bigger projects often use feasibility studies, as funders demand that they be fairly sure that the project will work. Certainly spending time thinking about the project is no bad thing, but the repeated questions and surveys cause justified (and well documented) resentment and suspicion. And there may also be some resentment from host governments, as such studies spend money on highly paid expatriates and sometimes come to nothing.

E5. The Pre-Planned Project

Often there is a tendancy on hearing of a project being done in another area to think "that sounds like a good idea". Starting such a "copy-cat" project, without examining its feasibility or viability in the new setting, is hardly ever a good idea.

With refugees, in particular, the constraints, skills and markets are likely to vary widely. Luckily most refugee projects do look at these factors; though some training projects do adopt an international standard course on say "automobile maintenance" without looking at the market and the real maintenance needs of the area. If you cannot get new imported spare gaskets, you may need to teach people how to make them from cardboard, even if they do not last as long!

E6. So what process is most suitable?

Since none of the above approaches are ideal with refugees - you cannot copy other programmes and you cannot spend much time researching, what can you do? Our respondents gave some suggestions with a number of common points:

1. Use as much informally gathered information on the refugees, their skills, their needs, as is possible. This increases the "cultural understanding", without raising expectations. Those agencies already running other non-IG projects, start with advantages - an understanding of the culture and a degree of trust from the refugees - which often more than makes up for a lack of expertise, as is shown in the AICF and ARC case studies.
2. Use information from other similar projects, but test it very critically against the conditions you face. Many of the IG projects were started by people who had never worked in income-generation before; and their general advice was "use common sense".
3. When you do need specific information, design your questioning process to get that information only, preferably as informally as possible, to avoid getting the answers the refugees think you want. Often, having two similar or related questions, in different parts of the questioning process, checks the information. For example asking how much profit the business makes at one point and asking how much money remains after buying the supplies and paying other costs, at another point.
4. Whenever it is possible, have a pilot phase, experimental phase, initial trial period or some other way of not designing the project completely, before you start. Alternatively, use a process, like ACORD in Port Sudan, which continually re-examines the best way of doing things.

E7. Having decided on the process - what information is needed?

Having decided on your planning process, what is needed? Given that there is only likely to be a limited amount of time, it is important to gather only as much information, in the relevant areas, as is needed. Basically, there are four areas of information needed - political, social, commercial and project-related and these are dealt with in the following paragraphs. Remember the time-scale is also important in knowing what to look for. The next section F. deals with time-scales and related changes.

E8. The Political Information needed

The long-term prospects of the refugees must be considered, before planning anything else. The answers to such questions about the future are likely to be unclear and possibly contradictory, depending on who you ask. However, every field worker must have some thoughts on the likelihood and timing of the durable solutions, return, resettlement or integration. He or she must also look for any differences in the answers to these for different sub-groups of refugees. Sometimes, these questions cannot be asked openly and inferences have to be drawn.

The second main area of political information needed is how income-generating projects are viewed by the host government and the refugee administering agency. Are they seen as "good things": as a way of increasing the flow of aid to the host country, or are they viewed with suspicion since they may compete with local enterprises? It may be that some types of IG are viewed more favourably than others. Attitudes vary between countries and so a complete summary is impossible. But, without this understanding, it can be difficult to present the proposed project in its best light.

A third area which must not be ignored covers the regulations regarding refugee income-generation, i.e. taxes, employment conditions, land ownership, the use of common land and trading restrictions.

E9. The Social/Cultural Information needed

Our respondents agreed that it is vitally important to know the main and subsiduary skills of the refugees and the levels of competence in those skills. Independently three respondents suggested that such information should be collected at the initial registration of refugees, as it is much easier to collect then. Such a skills list can be used for relief tasks, but really is fundamental to planning appropriate IG programmes and in starting them earlier.

It may also be possible at the initial registration to find out the refugees' level of education and whether they are from a rural of urban background - section Q., on choosing the participants of the programme discusses the importance of this information.

The cultural background of the refugees has already been emphasized, in section A4. and elsewhere. For example, in planning projects, certain cultural information is very useful. This information includes knowledge of the different subgroups, particularly those with special occupations, such as potter or metal worker castes. Religious or cultural practices, may affect the project directly, and it also necessary to understand sources of potential rivalry between the groups. The AICF case study shows how carefully they took this last point, recording 53 such groups.

The last area of cultural information needed is knowledge of the links between the refugees and the local people. According to our questionnaire replies, if there are small numbers of refugees having family links in the area, then they can obtain useful support. With large numbers of refugees, as for example in Pakistan or Somalia, (though not for all refugees), then the links with local people make them initially welcome. However, resentment builds up over time - especially if locals are not assisted. If there are no links, at all, then refugees often try harder, as they have to succeed.

E10. The Commercial Information needed

Most IG projects must be based on some commercial information; this includes even relief substitution, since the price that has to be paid may have to be compared to an international tender. The following checklist is taken from a number of books and studies, of which some deal with refugees.

The Situation Now:
- what income-generation is already happening in the area/camp?
- what problems are people experiencing?
- how did they get started?
- what is stopping people from starting businesses?
- do people have skills they are not using?

The Resources Available:
- what skills, in production/service/management/training/ supervision are available?
- what natural resources are available and accessible? This is especially important for rural and low-skilled refugees.
- what raw materials, either imported or transported from another part of the country, are available locally?
- are land and/or buildings available?

The Product or Service:
- what do the refugees know how to do?
- what products or services, which can use the resources available are not being done? (Or not being done adequately?)
- are the products or services exactly right for the market? (Can the design or quality be changed to suit the market better?)

The Market:
- is there an existing market for the proposed product or service?
- if there is an existing demand, who is satisfying it at the moment, and how does the new proposal satisfy it more effectively.
- if there is not a demand, why not?
- is the market with refugees, local people or a distant market and how does this affect the proposed activity?
- if a product: what are the likely production, selling costs and profits and how often do people buy them? Is a substitute possible?
- if a service: how many similar services exist, how many do they serve, what levels of profit do they make?
- if it is a new product or service, is there something similar, how successful is it, how far away is it?
- where is the best site to sell the product or service?
- how can the proposed customers best be informed about the product or service?

Is it Viable? (Remember to check all figures independently):
- are the necessary skills available, good enough (practical, financial and management skills)? If not, where and how can training be obtained?
- what capital equipment is needed? How much?
- what working capital or initial cash is needed? Could anything be hired, rather than bought outright?
- what starting materials are needed? How much?
- Are delays in getting materials or equipment likely? For how long and how does this affect the proposal?
- what are the other costs, such as rent, electricity, licenses, staff, transportation, administration?
- what is the rate of inflation expected to be? How does this affect the business?
- how much can be expected to be sold for what price and when will the money be received? Or what is the average turnover in a week/month? (There is a tendancy to be optimistic!)
- how much profit and reserves are needed? (Check expected profit against what others make (Again watch out for optimism)
- Is It Viable? (It is worth getting a second opinion)

Is it a Group Business? (Remember there is a preference for individual businesses)
- How is it organized?
- Who decides the division of responsibilities, working hours and salaries?
- How are problems of illness or disputes sorted out?

Other questions which concern production and stock control - do they give credit, seasonal variations and many other things that may need thought at the planning stage or as the business starts. This is a matter of personal judgement, and this list only covers the initial viability, not the continuing process of improving a business.

E11. The Project-Related Information needed

This information is divided into two related parts: the administrative details and the local staff needed.

<u>Administrative details</u>
We have written of the need for flexibility, experimentation and the advantages of an informal approach. There are nevertheless regulations, which must be observed, in the interests of the refugees, the local and expatriate staff, and the host countries who have generously offered asylum.

a) Agreements - what is required by the host government and funding agencies and occasionally co-ordinating agencies.
b) Monitoring - what monitoring and evaluation procedures are to be built into the project?
c) Unforeseen circumstances - what contingency plans must be made for the project failing to achieve its objectives; for drastic changes in the situation, for accidents or for criminal acts?

d) Expatriate staff - most agencies know the sort of staff they want and the conditions they offer, but are there anything special requirements for this particular project with refugees?

e) Financial arangements - how will money be sent to the project for local purchases and what discretion will local field staff have? How can management at all levels ensure that the financial arrangements make it easier to spend money on local resources than on foreign ones, whether they be staff or supplies.

f) Logistics - often the refugee affected areas are not in easy places to work, so what special changes need to be made? Sometimes, this is forgotten and programmes spend their first few months trying to set up communications, supply lines or other logistical support.

<u>Local staff</u>
We have already discussed how a project can use its own purchasing power to benefit the refugee community or local area; the most obvious way of doing this, which can also bring other benefits apart from wages, is by employing local, (non-expatriate) staff or preferably refugees or local people. There are a number of issues which must be settled and questions asked:

a) How many local staff will be required, what skills will they need to have and where and how can they be trained? The skills available and the length of the working day certainly affect the numbers and maybe the training of the staff needed.

b) Will the local staff have to be chosen from a number of different subgroups, so they can match the refugee community in terms of language and acceptability?

c) How many female local staff will be needed, will they require special training, will the local culture permit unaccompanied women to act as field officers? Should more women be employed to overcome discrimination or lack of skills?

d) What special opportunities need to be made available for handicapped people to obtain jobs with the project? This is especially desirable and may help the project relate to handicapped refugees in general.

e) Should the project hire rather more people than necessary and ask them to work less hours for less money in the interests of spreading wages and training amongst a greater number? If the working day is short and the pay low, why not employ more?

f) What role will the local staff be expected to play after the foreign assistance has been withdrawn? How can the right local staff be selected at the outset to ensure that something remains when the project is withdrawn?

g) Who will actually employ the local staff? In some countries staff are selected, seconded or appointed by the government, and if so what effect does this have?

h) How can the project move towards becoming an independent, self-sustaining activity by gradually increasing local staff participation and management? As with other aspects, we would advocate a gradual change, with local staff taking on more responsibility in the hope of becoming an independent agency. But this cannot be done quickly.

i) In training the local staff, is there anything to recommend initially? Because these sorts of programme are relatively new to refugees (and often local people) it seems that on-the-job and internal courses should be built into many of the local staffs' jobs and if possible a planned staff development programme should be begun.

F. TIME-SCALES

F1. What sort of Time-scales?

So far in this book, "time-scales" has been used as a shorthand for a number of different effects which happen at different times. When does the relief phase end? How long do each of the phases between relief and flexible development last? How long should projects exist? Unfortunately the difficulty in answering these questions, indicates the fundamental dilemma of refugees unable to move towards one of the "durable solutions".

"When" is the question on everyones' lips, but the refugees do not know, the host government does not know and nor do the the agencies. Some refugees, even some agencies, wait, not willing to do anything, while others will try anything; neither produce constructive answers to a difficult situation. We suggest here, that it is possible to plan in these uncertain conditions.

F2. When does the Relief Phase end and I.G. projects begin?

The physical answer to the question is: "when the food and water supplies are stabilized". If a few refugees are starting to set up their small enterprises, without any assistance, this can be a valuable indicator that the time is ripe to start projects to help others do the same. This seems true of both urban, self-settled refugees and camp-based refugees.

According to the replies, this stage takes place somewhere between six months and a year after the refugees arrive. There also seems to be a longer period, when many refugees who will evenyually start their own businesses try and build up some capital by working (35%), or by selling possessions brought from their previous homes (24%), or by borrowing from various sources (60%). These figures include those whose capital came from a combination of activities. During this period, the refugees also try to build up business contacts.

Meanwhile, the agencies are also studying the situation and making recommendations. But this is a slow process, so the first IG projects happen 2-3 years after arrival, but preparations by the agencies and the refugees started a year before. As this process is better understood, especially by the funding agencies, a quicker response may become possible.

F3. How long do projects last and can they be too late?

The average IG project in our survey had been prepared for one year, has been operating for three years and is continuing.

According to some respondents, some IG programmes must start before four years after the refugees arrival, otherwise the dependancy factor makes starting very difficult. However, none of the business assistance programmes studied began before the fourth year (in Pakistan, Somalia and Sudan). So perhaps Phase D, in Figure 3. - the phase when the business assistance and employment bureau projects start - can be fixed at about the fourth year. None of the other phases can be fixed to a time-scale, but the order seems to remain the same, in the very different countries and situations.

CHOOSING AND RUNNING INCOME GENERATING PROJECTS
(Sections G. to O.)

G. CHOOSING THE TYPE OF IG ASSISTANCE PROJECT

G1. Introduction to Choosing

The choice may have already been made. The refugees or another agency might have suggested a particular type of project - the UNHCR in Pakistan gave a lead and support to several agencies to begin some IG projects.

Or the project might start from other work the agency is doing. For instance, several health agencies began helping refugees to cultivate small gardens, initially to improve nutrition, with the hope that it might also improve the refugees' income.

Alternatively, an agency might be especially skilled in a particular type of project. For example, Partnership for Productivity specialised in business assistance programmes, running many such programmes with nationals of developing countries before starting with refugees in Somalia. Or the Ockenden Venture, which had run relief substitution programmes in Thailand, then began them in Pakistan.

This "natural" form of choice is very valid and has generally worked; though we would recommend a look at other types of IG as well. The rest of this section is really for agencies and their staff who are interested in IG, but who do not know where to begin, or for those who would like to examine how choices can be made.

G2. The First Thoughts

As suggested earlier, in the sections on the types of IG projects and on time-scales, the first two questions to ask are: "how near the refugees are to the relief phase?" and "what is the political situation in that country?" It is as wrong to start development style projects near the relief phase as it is to start relief-style handouts, if the refugees are already starting more developmental activities.

With regard to the political situation, those poor counties have been remarkably generous in accepting large numbers of refugees, but there will always be some restrictions, usually dependent on quite understandable conditions in those countries. Our respondents suggested that "all countries have some xenophobia, and perhaps these are less so, than some industrialized or developed countries." However, all countries set up bureaucracies and rules (whether written or not), and these conditions usually restrict income-generating activity, in some way. Since assistance agencies both need and often actively seek government support, they must achieve a delicate balance in relation to the rules which appear to constrain refugee enterprises. In general, our respondents felt that the best way to overcome this type of restriction was to "advance tactfully until told to stop". If the advance is genuinely tactful, the order to stop may never come.

To introduce another political point - do the host governments benefit from having refugees? Having refugees usually brings in cheap food, it provides employment and it brings in foreign exchange - so the answer is "yes", initially. However, valuable land is taken up, and experienced staff are not used for national development. As the flow of aid declines, competition grows between refugees and local people.

One respondent wrote that "[the host country] is economically gaining at the moment, but may lose in the long run". It certainly is the case that some host countries do obstruct the process from relief to flexible development, for these sorts of reasons. So, we suggest agencies should advance towards flexible development, but be careful not to create a situation where the host government has to make a decision on how far they will allow that advance.

In the long term, history suggests that many refugee communities have provided a valuable stimulus to economic development in many forms. This is not only true of refugee movements that took place many years ago, such as the Huguenots or the Jews, but it can also be claimed that the Ugandan Asians in the United Kingdom or the Vietnamese and others in the United States and many other groups, who have moved from poor countries to rich ones, have provided a valuable stimulus for entrepreneurship. It remains to be seen whether the far larger numbers of refugees from one poor country, who appear likely to stay in another poor country, will have a similar effect on their new hosts; but in a modest way, income-generation support activities can and do contribute to this optimistic outcome.

G3. Grants or Loans?

Progress from relief to development is often matched by a move from grants to loans. Immediately after the relief phase people find it difficult to ask for money from the refugees and most assistance is in the form of grants or free equipment. Later on, refugees become capable of repaying some part of what they have received and thus assist others; they are still, nevertheless, poor and it is felt appropriate to make interest-free loans, instead of grants.

As the refugee economy becomes more established, then loans are introduced which include charges or interest, usually at the same level as the loans available to the local population, so the refugees are seen not to be special cases any more. Assistance agencies may find it difficult to move through these stages, since the host government, donors and other agencies often argue that all refugees are poor and should not be asked to repay loans, and should certainly not be charged fees or interest.

The reader is referred to some of the books in the bibliography, which go into interest charges in some detail; generally speaking, it can be shown that even quite high interest rates make very little difference to the types of enterprises that refugees are likely to start, and can make a very great difference to the self-sustainability of the assistance operation itself.

In many countries, traders who borrow less than $100, just for a day or two, to buy goods and then sell them again are charged one per cent a day. The woman trading vegetables or the man buying scrap metal wonder how the lender can make a profit - the lender gets a single dollar and they make ten or more dollars. However banks may be envious of the 365% or more interest earned a year. Is this exploitative - the men and women borrowing don't think so, the money lender or agency have much administration to do each day? What do you think?

Some local agencies in these countries, have borrowed from banks or government sources, added their administration costs, and the resultant annual interest of 30% or more is still cheaper than other credit sources available to the poorest people. AND the agency is self-sustaining!

G4. What Next?

Once the refugees have been "placed" along the time-scale between relief and flexible development, and the official environment offered by the host country has been assessed, readers may find it useful to study Figure 3. and relate this to their own situation. This will make it easier to choose the right type of project.

The preceding sections A. to F. give details of the issues to consider before starting; and if more details are needed about a particular type, then refer to sections H. to O. In general, a careful formulation of the goals and objectives, should be the most relevant (Section D.) in the agencies' choice of project.

There was a second reason for entitling this section "what next?" In the introduction to the book, we said that after the relief phase, people asked the question "what now?". And the answer was given as income-generation. Now the questions and answers can be more specific, "what sort of IG project is the most suitable" or "what is the next stage or decision".

G5. Agency Roles in Assisting Income-generation

Each type of IG project covers a wide range and degree of agency intervention; from an isolated piece of advice to a refugee on improving his or her business, to the agency paying refugees' wages and marketing products. Such differences in the agencies' interventions between one programme and another do not necessarily reflect greater "success" or "failure". That was clearly shown by the study, despite comments that it is impossible to mix relief work and self-sufficiency programmes. It is possible to have intermediate positions, but the direction should always be towards a development style.

Field workers must think through the style and amount of assistance that the different types of income-generation programme imply, and they must be sure they and their colleagues can provide both. To give one respondent's view on this difficult task - "Flexibility is the Key".

H. RELIEF SUBSTITUTION

H1. Introduction

By relief substitution we mean projects set up and managed by relief agencies, which employ refugees to make, or occasionally grow, products for the use of the refugees themselves. We call this "substitution", because refugee-made goods are substituted for imported items, so that the refugees obtain the benefit of the goods themselves, of the income created and of the self-esteem of employment. Sometimes, such goods are bought from traders or the government in the host country, which is preferable to importation, but not as good as the refugees producing for themselves. In rare cases, it may be possible for some refugees to produce goods for refugees in other countries, such as Afghani refugee quilts can be used by refugees in other countries with cold climates.

There is a far wider scope for this activity than is presently practised, particularly after the emergency phase, when such goods need to be sent in large numbers, quickly. Perhaps this importation continues from habit or from having cheaper international prices than refugee production costs, or perhaps the time and effort involved dissuades agencies from trying to give refugees the benefit of this type of project.

However, of those projects that have started, the commonest items produced were cloth tents, quilts, blankets or clothes or school items, bags and uniforms - the list from the survey is in section P. Below are some examples of other items that could be produced by the refugees, taken from the questionnaires or from background reading. Although construction projects are usually defined as development investment, there are a few cases that fit more easily in relief substitution:

Construction
- local buildings, instead of pre-fabs or tents.
- local lime, instead of cement.
- hand dug wells with local reinforcing, material instead of using imported machines or materials.

Medical
- contracts for distilled water, local cotton wool, highly nutritious plants, instead of vitamin supplements.

Standard relief goods (not already mentioned)
- clothes, utensils, water-jugs, shoes, anything else?

Agency and expatriate needs - not directly for refugees, but again substituting for imported goods:- buying a cow or chickens to supply milk and eggs, giving seeds to get fresh vegetables and any other ideas?

Two main reasons were given for not giving refugees these opportunities. Firstly, the lack of local resources - we can sympathise with that problem. Secondly, the speed of delivery - while it might take time to organize the refugees, it is nearly always true that relief goods themselves do not come quickly and sending raw materials might be as quick. One interesting comment on this by a respondent was "Agencies cannot _risk_ leaving some tasks to the refugees, even if it is theoretically good for development".

H2. Statistics

Five per cent of the IG programmes covered in our survey could be classified as relief substitution, involving fourteen projects carried out by eight agencies, mostly within Pakistan. Though there may be many more, hidden within non-IG agencies - health, education, construction and water programmes being obvious examples.

Two of the agencies, running four projects, gave us fairly complete details of their activities. They are employing a total of 4,510 refugees for $1,828,000 to make goods for 112,610 refugees. This gives an annual cost per employee of $405 and per recipient of $16.

We also have some data from the UNHCR 1987 budget for Pakistan; there are six agencies carrying out nine projects and employing 940 refugees for $1,678,232 to make goods for 542,000 refugees. This gives an annual cost per employee of $1,785 (see Evaluation, section Y., for more sensible comparisons) and per recipient of $3. This low figure is mostly because the data included a well-digging programme benefitting 260,000 refugees.

It seems surprising that only seven of the seventeen agencies replying to our survey question actually claimed to use their own purchasing power to benefit refugees by buying from them. Similarly, only 19% of the 124 refugee businesses questioned sold anything to agencies, and none of them claimed that the agencies were their main customers.

Given the enormous range of goods and services required by the refugees after the emergency phase and the substantial market of the agencies and their staff, it would appear there is great potential in buying more from refugee sources.

H3. Other Comments

As a way of starting to bring money into the camp or refugee-affected area, providing jobs and using the aid money where it is needed, there is a lot to commend relief substitution, particularly during or soon after the relief phase. Perhaps every agency and every staff member should "audit" their purchases and ensure that everything possible is bought from refugee, or at least local, sources. However as time goes on, few agencies make any attempt to hand over, or to teach the product-management skills - getting supplies, pricing, marketing, etc. The situation is very much "give a man a fish, you feed him for one day", but what happens if the agency leaves or the people go back home, can they expect another similar programme in their home country? One respondent felt that jobs were more important, so if the project is going well why change it? We have given the reasons why not.

Many of these projects are carried out in supervised workshops, for supervision and quality control reasons, which means they are difficult to change into independent businesses. There is the question of who will own them and how to train the managers. With a little thought beforehand, individual businesses or small groups could reduce the managerial problems on a later handover.

One advantage and simultaneously a disadvantage of relief substitution programmes is that they only last as long as the contract; they can start quickly, but they do not carry on producing an income after the agency has left. They, in common with other IG programmes started immediately after the relief phase, can produce a ratio of assistance cost to first year return of less than one (see section Y.). Which means perhaps that one of the important goals of development - self-sustainability - is not being thought through properly.

I. DEVELOPMENT INVESTMENT

I1. Introduction to Development Investment

These IG projects hope to provide essential services needed to assist the development of the refugees and often the local population as well, with for example, water and road infrastructure. It is not easy to discuss this type of activity generally, as there are so many possible, diverse things which could be a good investment.

These projects are usually able to generate a great deal of employment, especially for the unskilled, and so are very important in acheiving a balanced outlook on services for the whole refugee population. Most other IG programmes, except for those specializing in training, do tend to assist the skilled and semi-skilled. Hence the value of these projects is in the investment created, such as a better road built, and in the employment created, rather than any income created now or in the future.

There are two main areas of Development Investment - Infrastructural and Environmental projects. In our survey we identified construction, maintenance, roads, water supply and irrigation under infrastructural projects. Under environmental projects we found dams, erosion control, fuel-saving cookers and ovens, trees and forestry projects. Often both types are so large or diverse that they come under headings other than "income-generation" - which does seem to imply an element of "small-scale".

I2. Statistics

We found 3% each of environmental and infrastructural projects in our survey, though again more might exist, but not be thought to be "income-generating", as the main goal is the activity itself, not the IG aspects.

In section A5. we analyzed briefly one project of each, but as all are so different, it seemed appropriate to give details of these in the short case studies following.

I3. Infrastructure Case Study - The World Bank in Pakistan

This large afforestation and irrigation programme was set for a three year period from the beginning of 1984 to the end of 1986. The World Bank funded this infrastructure programme primarily to provide employment for locals and and for refugees, who were expected to make up 70% of those involved. It was run by the Government of Pakistan and in addition to employment, its goals were to:

1. Restore the damage to Pakistan's ecology, resulting from the refugee presence.
2. Generate viable economic resources in refugee affected areas, by a number of short-term projects. The projects identified had to be:
    - technically viable, with a 12% rate of return
    - labour intensive
    - in close proximity to existing refugee villages

There were two main implementors, with different projects - a final evaluation was not available, but by the end of September 1986, the results were mostly on target.

AFORESTATION - run by the Chief Conservator of Forests
In two sites were: nurseries, afforestation, road side plantation, soil conservation works, roads, bridle paths, pasture management, fruit orchards and mazri sowing.

These projects were budgeted at $4 million, and by September 443,648 man-days had been worked: 85% by refugees, representing 69% of total expenditure.

IRRIGATION - run by the Chief Engineer of Irrigation
In 79 sites various flood protection works and canal patrol roads were undertaken; 68 sites were completed by the end of September.

These projects were budgeted at $5.5 million, and by September 561,646 man-days had been worked: 79% by refugees, representing 56% of total expenditure.

Conclusions: The project seems to have been a success, despite bureaucratic and administrative difficulties and there is a second project planned. The 12% rate of return is calculated over 15 years and also seems to be on target. This represents a slower rate of return, than the other case studies, as it indicates a ratio of assistance cost to wage income of about 1:0.12. But because of the large numbers employed and the long-term environmental benefits, this must be judged to be a very valuable programme.

I4. Environment Case Study - The GTZ Fuel-Saving Project in Pakistan

Deutsche Gesellschaft Fuer Technische Zusammenarbeit (GTZ) have a Domestic Energy Saving Project, a Technical Training Project and Construction Teams in Pakistan, helping the Afghan refugees. Here we will deal with the first. This project comes under the heading of an environmental, development investment project, because of its main goals below. But it is a mixed IG project, giving training in metal and clay work to produce metal and ceramic stoves and ovens, and helping independent businesses in clay, metal-work and bakeries with loans. The projects two main objectives are:-

1) To reduce the pressure on forests in the North-West Frontier Province (NWFP) by fuel-saving domestic food-processing equipment.

2) To generate income by establishing independent clay and metal workshops and bakeries.

The programme started in January 1985 and will continue to the end of 1988. It costs $350,000 per year and had two expatriate staff originally, now one. They work in over 50 camps with about 80 staff and in the last year (to November 1986), they helped 76 businesses with an average loan of $156, repaid monthly. They estimate that 30% are in arrears, with a 20% default rate.

GTZ themselves contracted about one third of these businesses to produce the stoves and ovens. GTZ have sold about 20,000 so far, and have now reached a rate of 800 each month. Because of Purdah, they have evolved a strategy whereby a male demonstrator goes to a public place and shows how fast the cookers cook compared to a traditional clay horseshoe-shaped cooker. They sell to the men for 50 rupees (about $3) - an average income is 1-2,000 rupees a month. A woman demonstrator then goes to the man's home and demonstrates to the women there, or she goes to the Primary Health Units and meets women directly. These cookers save 30% of the fuel used by the traditional cookers. A fitting pot is included in the price.

The ovens are free, but the refugees have to provide the base of clay or bricks. They are only made for groups of three or four families to bake the traditional nan bread, and by doing this, up to 70% of the fuel can be saved. This is because not only are they more efficient, but each family saves the costs of heating the oven from cold. GTZ also have the same programme with Pakistanis, but it is smaller. They have a radio/television campaign to help the promotion, and they hope to create a steady market so the production centres can also become independent.

In the 1987 proposal, GTZ hope to employ 90 producers to make stoves and ovens to benefit 28,680 refugee families by a reduction in fuel expenditure of 40 - 80 rupees a month. This is at a cost of $109,000 and excludes expatriate staff. In 1985, this was calculated to have saved $172,800 worth of fuel wood at $20 per ton.

Using these figures, rather than the initial ones, which included high starting costs, assuming total cost at $140,000, the calculated saving is $1,290,600. So the project assistance cost to saving ratio is 1:9.2, which is very high. The same amount of money could, of course, be lost from the income of refugee wood sellers. Despite this complication, the project does represent a great saving for poor families and probably a steady income for 90 people. But perhaps the most important contribution is to saving the forests and wood-stocks of Pakistan.

15. Concluding Comments

We noted earlier, these infrastructure projects are not designed primarily to generate or save income, although they can do so quite well. Our main advice is to try and ensure that refugees do, over time, take on all the project functions, including management. The planning for this should include training the workers, as in the GTZ project, then they can become self-sufficient. Even the construction projects can be designed in this way, although this is not usual.

J. INCOME-ADDING STARTERS

J1. Introduction

Making small grants of money or equipment, or very occasionally small loans, to start a small project, is one good way of introducing an agency to an area. It also acts as a way of collecting knowledge about the many aspects of refugee life, without asking questions. However, the likelihood of it being an efficient use of money is low. Usually such grants are made without much investigation of the refugees' skills, the markets or the most appropriate form of assistance. Remember the tale of the dying White Leghorn chickens, where inappropriate "gifts" were given, because of agencies' lack of knowledge. But refugees, like anyone else, are unlikely to turn down a free gift, even if it is not very useful!

If you look at the 112 trades in section P. assisted by different organisations as income-adding starters, training projects or independent businesses, most of these businesses could have been assisted in any one of the three ways. What determines that the choice should be an income-adding starter?

Firstly, there is an element of uncertainty: are the refugees staying? Since these income-adding starters are begun soon after the relief phase, there is still that doubt - and planning is difficult without a known time-scale.

Secondly, it is just after the relief phase, so the refugees in camps or towns are getting aid free (usually) and to suddenly charge for aid can strike the wrong psychological note. If loans are used, these start later than the grants and are usually interest or charge free.

Thirdly, these projects are often started by agencies which are generally not mainly involved in IG, so the budgets may be small, and possibly the staff not experienced in this field. They may also have very little time for supervision. It may well be a matter of luck for the agency to find a trade with some potential, such as a vegetable that is popular and nutritious, or an expert in an appropriate activity, such as chicken raising.

Finally, even if the agency is involved in IG, then these projects are used as experiments to test such things as group organization, markets, traditional business organization, wages or profit margins. The Quaker group in Somalia used the chicken and house garden projects in this way. In any case, the amounts of aid are likely to be small and there is not a great expectation of success since the refugees are likely to be emerging from their ordeal and still dependent in many ways.

J2. Statistics

Twenty-five of the 149 agencies studied (17%) have run, or are running, income-adding starters with an average assistance of $85. However, we do not have many more details. They are usually one-off grants, the results are not evaluated, no income figures are estimated and the grants are given on hopes of viability, rather than analysis. These projects seem to occur more frequently, where there are small numbers of refugees rather than a big influx, and 13 of the agencies are church organizations (55% of sample).

J3. Comments

There are relatively large numbers of income-adding starter projects, despite the low chances of success; why should this be? One reason may be that both the refugees and the field staff of the agencies feel that they should be doing something constructive as soon as possible after the relief phase. Therefore a quick, cheap, easy to organize (supposedly) and small-scale solution is needed.

According to the 1986 review of UNHCR-assisted IG projects in Pakistan, 11,000 kg of vegetable seeds were distributed to refugees. The yields were "400-500 times lower than standard values", for example chilli seeds should give a yield of 2,000kg per hectare, but the actual yield was 5kg per hectare. The reasons given for this were "poor quality of seeds...inappropriate time of planting (lack of advice and supervision)....inappropriate soil conditions and water availability....insufficient knowledge of refugees on growing".

Unfortunately similar comments can and have been made of some vegetable and chicken projects in other parts of the world. However, on the positive side, many small income-adding starter projects have either worked well, or at least provided the information to enable the design of much better assistance programmes. In looking for the reasons for success, it seems that such projects are really very small businesses and need a minimum study of viability and levels of support. Given these factors, they can and do work, usually where someone is there to give time and assistance.

K. BASIC SKILL UTILIZATION

K1. Introduction

"Basic skill utilization" is a general term, that we have coined to include a wide range of different activities. It is a collection of those projects that use the traditional or existing skills of the refugees, but which are not normally described as businesses. Generally they are of two main types, either agricultural schemes or village craft schemes.

Agricultural schemes are often under separate government, UNHCR or other co-ordinating bodies' departments to those for income-generating projects. Very small farming or gardening projects are usually put with income-adding starters (like vegetable gardens and chickens). Agricultural schemes are often very similar to local agricultural development schemes that have nothing to do with refugees. For these reasons, we are not dealing with them in detail.

Despite not usually classifying agricultural schemes as income-generating, some 13 of the 149 IG projects (9%) were classified as agricultural. They ranged from giving seeds and a few hand tools, to full-scale irrigation, cultivation and marketing projects. The only particular issue for refugees was that of land usage. In Sudan, Somalia and Pakistan some of the refugees who used to farm have now rented land or worked as occasional farm labourers. Sometimes land that looked unused became owned, as soon as refugees or agencies took an interest in it. These traditional claims can be difficult to prove and cause many arguments.

Village craft schemes are a far more familiar part of income-generation activity. Although classification is not easy as they can often look like either relief substitution or small businesses. However village craft schemes are common and there are distinctive features - the element of tradition, the use of local materials, and the possibility of piecework or part-time work. But such projects can have many difficulties - probably everyone from the area can make the same handicrafts, so there is little local market or the crafts are not of a good enough quality to export.

K2. Statistics

Thirteen village crafts projects made up 9% of the survey. They ranged from the very small with just ten leatherworkers, to the very large, which involved 1,200 women, mostly widows, producing handicrafts. The products also varied from simple mats to very beautiful carpets, with prices to match. It is, in fact both difficult and dangerous to generalize about this form of income-generation.

K3. Village Craft Programme Improvements

Traditional crafts are an immediately attractive possibility, especially to outsiders, The refugees have the necessary skills, the raw materials are often locally available and the finished products look attractive and marketable, particularly abroad, because they have an instant association with the refugees. However, there are many dangers in this form of activity and it may be useful to point out a few of them:

a) Quality control - because many people can make traditional items, only those of the best quality will sell internationally or even on the local market. Some agencies overcome this by only involving the most skilled workers, while others insist on a strict training and supervision approach. Other agencies allow and encourage refugees to make items, but stress that they buy only those items that pass a quality test. The choice of tactics depends on the objectives of the programme, is it to help a particular group, is it to create employment or is it to help independent businesses?

b) Marketing - even with the best quality products there may be marketing problems. Handicrafts rely on traditional skills, which often involve women who are away from the places where such items might be sold. If they were in their home country and their own culture, there are handicraft sellers (men and women), who buy from the homes and sell in the markets. Agencies often take over this role for the refugees - in Pakistan 6 of the 14 agencies helping village crafts were mainly involved in marketing. Those outside agencies that market refugee products internationally play a delicate role with the host government and people. Competition must be avoided with local products and the agency must understand the regulations governing export or exchange control.

The marketing role is a complex one. It not only involves understanding the business of improving the sales and market sector, it is also a two-way process. Those helping with market assistance need to return to the producers and change the design, size, colour or whatever is necessary to help sales. But, since the product is traditional and has always been made that way, it can be difficult to explain why a change is needed.

c) The questions of subsidy and self-sufficiency - all aid programmes contain a degree of subsidy. The questions are how much, how long and for what? For village craft programmes, some agency staff visit producers, find a product and start selling it. Soon afterwards, people start comparing the level of sales with the cost of the programme. The staff are, in effect, carrying out the marketing task, and the actual costs of the staff, transport, packaging and so on may be enormous when compared with the price that has been paid to the producer. But by this stage it is too late, the producers are used to being paid by the agency, having a free collection service and easy payment and not spending time trying to sell their products.

To get around this problem, UNHCR Pakistan and others take into account the objective of being self-supporting at the beginning. As well as the numbers of participants and the costs, UNHCR look for the "break-even point". This is the point when all the costs (wages/salaries, a 10% depreciation on equipment, costs of materials, rents and a percentage of the administrative and management costs) are covered by the margin on sales. The initial high costs of expatriate administration and training are not included in the calculation, but a date is set for the expatriates to finish as soon as the break-even point is reached. If the margin on the sales is higher than these added costs, then the project has reached self-sufficiency. This is a difficult, but worthy goal and it is not known how many passed this condition, introduced in 1986.

L. VOCATIONAL TRAINING AND PRODUCTION

L1. Introduction

Vocational training was the commonest form of assistance provided by the agencies in our survey at 26% of the sample. The level of the skills taught varies greatly. At one end of the scale are the relatively simple and inexpensive crafts, such as weaving, tailoring or leatherwork and at the other end are the complex and capital-intensive trades, like automobile mechanics or printing technology. These extremes are indicated by the data, given in section A5. where the training cost varies from $25 to $1,775 per trainee per year.

There are enormous numbers of different trades and it would be impossible to go into detail on each one here; in any case it is usually possible to find good handbooks on most trades. We have therefore emphasized the organizational aspects of training in this section. Some points on "entrepreneurship training" are dealt with in section N.

L2. Training for Business or Training for its own sake?

It is very easy to set up training for its own sake, and to forget that the aim is to provide a skill for use in employment or self-employment after training. Training is a tangible, and always acceptable activity, with measurable results in terms of numbers trained. It is often tempting to introduce training courses in answer to the question "what do we do next?", rather than plan programmes with genuine, long-term objectives. There seem to be three common mistakes:

a) Thinking a need is the same as a job -
If there is a need for a skill, this does not mean that people trained in that skill will have work. One agency saw a need for plumbers and started a training course for plumbers. However, on completion of the course there was no money to buy tools, the existing plumbers did not want to employ the refugees as they might be future competition, and the refugees had not been trained in business, so they could not start on their own. One or more of these mistakes have been made by many agencies. It is worse for refugees, who may have to overcome cultural or language difficulties. An initial sensitive employment survey, can avoid these problems.

b) My standard or yours?
Although everybody wants a higher standard of skill and raising standards in poorer countries is always helpful, it does not always help employment. We have seen electric sewing machines in tailoring schools in countries with very poor or non-existent electricity supplies; and automobile mechanics shown how to fit new spare parts which are unavailable on the local market, instead of learning to repair old parts.

Some agencies, rather than train people themselves, pay local businesses to take on apprentices or trainees. This is often cheaper than setting up a training institution, it ensures the standard of training is locally relevant, brings some money into the local businesses and helps forge links with the local communities. Obviously though, problems with the standard of training and any hint of exploitation must be avoided in these cases.

c) Training for a job as well as a trade -

People trained in practical skills alone may need other help. As well as all the technical aspects of a trade, every course should include either help with finding jobs or training in being self-employed. Both should include legal and financial aspects.

L3. Training as Production Units

It is generally accepted that training is more effective, if the trainees make things or provide services which are sold to real customers, rather than merely produced as exercises. Apprenticeship-type schemes do this automatically, but classroom-type training has to find production outlets - like the ARC Training Centre, producing items for the medical programme.

Sometimes, groups of trainees are trained together to eventually become independent production units. The Quakers did this with the tie-dye project in Somalia and though it may be a lengthy process for what started as a training class to become a viable business, it can be one way of overcoming the problems of employment, once training is completed.

We would always advocate that training is directed towards gaining employment or self-employment and that during the changes from the relief to flexible development, training should become more and more production and employment orientated. For refugees soon after the relief phase, the uncertainties of the future and the factors of the "portability" of the trade can make such employment and production orientations more difficult, but certainly not impossible.

L4. Evaluation

It is very difficult to evaluate training, since the real results are not evident until a year or more after the training has been completed, and its effectiveness can be measured by the numbers employed or self-employed. Training itself is an investment, or cost, and employment is the return; indicators such as the numbers trained, numbers passing tests or costs per trainee, are of some value, but are purely provisional. Unlike most forms of assistance, training can only be evaluated some time after it has been completed for a given trainee. In our evaluation section Y., we suggest that a year afterwards is suitable.

M. BUSINESS STARTERS

M1. Introduction

Business starter projects, like the tool kits given to skilled Afghan refugees shown in the AICF case study, are extremely successful at the right time: too early and the refugees are not ready or just take the item, say "Thank you very much", and do nothing; too late and the entrepreneurs have already started.

Assistance by giving business starter grants of money or equipment (or small charge free loans) is at the mid point between relief aid and development aid - it encourages people to start a business, not just an income-adding activity, but it is still a "hand-out". Later, these projects must change - probably the agency should determine a date, such as two years from starting, in which to change to a more advice orientated service. This service would be coupled with the possibility of loans with charges for larger amounts than the starter amount (a business assistance programme). There are three reasons for this:.

1. The businesses may need more advanced assistance by this stage.

2. Most such businesses, which are able to use the level of basic starter help, would have already started.

3. The psychological and practical move should be away from relief-style assistance towards a developmental style.

These business starter projects could possibly be seen to be between income adding starters and business assistance. The following figures only apply to rural refugees in poorer countries:

TABLE 6. Comparing Income-adding Starters to Business Starters to Business Assistance Projects

Relief Stage
↓

	Average Cost	Free Equipment?	Feasibility Study?
Income Adding Starters	$85	Yes	No
BUSINESS STARTERS	$253	Mostly	Yes
Business Assistance	$901	No	In detail

↓
Flexible Development Stage

M2. Statistics

Thirty-three of the 149 programmes studied (22%) were business starters and so were three of the five case studies. The majority of the list of 112 different businesses mentioned in section P. were from organizations with business starter programmes. Whereas training or income-adding starter projects may try to restrict their scope of operation, business starter programmes try to deal with as many different types of business as possible.

M3. Other Comments

a) The cultural background seems very important for the success of these projects - see section A4. The success of these projects in Pakistan may be due, in large part, to the relatively skilled and highly entrepreneurial Afghan people.

b) The agencies in the business starter case studies managed to keep their staff and administration costs low compared to the costs of the assistance given to the refugees. But this ratio must be monitored regularly as it is not always so true for all programmes.

c) Some evaluation a year, or at least several months, after the assistance has ended, must be included - as programmes usually last for more than a year this should only prove difficult in the final year.

d) Business starters, by their nature, tend to help those with some skills already, who only need a helping hand to get started. Agencies must be aware that if they want to help groups or individuals who need more assistance, they must put in much more time with those refugees.

N. BUSINESS ASSISTANCE

N1. Introduction

These programmes are called by many different names, advice/loan schemes, business enterprise programmes and other combinations. Their similarities outweigh their differences; they all examine a business or a business proposal and try to help that business with tailor-made assistance, rather than give a standard assistance package. Only 6% of the refugee IG study were business assistance programmes. They are used more often with local people in poor countries than with refugees, but as refugees stay longer it can be expected there will be more programmes of this type.

As indicated in Figure 3., business assistance programmes indicate a crucial cross-over stage in that a host country has to accept some economic integration for such programmes to succeed. The giving of relatively large amounts of money (or helping their transfer) also indicates a change in the refugees' status. Perhaps for these reasons, not many refugee-affected countries have allowed these programmes. However, in line with our advice to "keep advancing tactfully, until told to stop", there are many sub-types of scheme and one or a combination could perhaps be adapted to different situations (see N3.).

N2. Statistics

Nine of the 149 programmes studied were the business assistance type. Unfortunately, the divisions into the eight types of IG programme were only made after the questionnaires were returned and the questions were not specific enough to outline an average business assistance programme. They all gave loans, and a tremendous range of non-financial assistance, and more details of these can be found in sections U. and V. respectively.

However, the analysis of the questionnaires did show the clear distinction between income-adding starters, business starters and business assistance - see Table 6. in section M. Basically, business assistance programmes give bigger loans, very few grants and much wider support to the businesses.

N3. Different Parts of a Business Assistance Programme

The most common forms of assistance are loans and advice, but the following list covers most of the possible elements of a business assistance programme:

a) Provision of loans, as appropriate to new/existing businesses, as part of a revolving loan fund, often with commercial or zero interest.
b) Providing advice on business problems, including feasibility studies.
c) The agency acts as guarantor for refugees applying to banks for loans.
d) Grant element in addition to loans for special groups/high risk businesses or those making new products.
e) Special facilities for particular sections of the population.
f) Extra assistance - help with business accomodation, getting supplies, marketing, legal permissions, packaging, importing machinery and in other ways.
g) Training - in entrepreneurship (see below), in practical skills (often through placements in local businesses, rather than in the classroom), or in business skills, like accounting, managing or marketing.

N4. Money or Advice?

Very often businesses can be helped with management advice rather than financial assistance, however it may be difficult for the agency to establish credibility if no material assistance is on offer. So frequently such programmes do start with loans and then go on to give the other assistance needed. There is always a danger with any business people, that they over-emphasize their need for finance and ignore their other problems. For refugees starting businesses, however, their priority may well be financial help. They are unlikely to have substantial funds of their own, their connections with the local community will tend to be weak or non-existent, they are likely to be outside the informal network which is so important in gaining credit and they have no guarantee for credit from other sources, such as banks or suppliers.

N5. Entrepreneurship Training or Selection

We found no such training, but some evidence of trying to select entrepreneurs amongst these programmes with refugees. In similar programmes not involving refugees, they are much more common. Without wishing to enter the debate on whether entrepreneurs are born with such skills or can be trained to acquire them, we would suggest that those interested in this refer to the bibliography at the back of the book.

N6. Other Comments

a) A grant element within a loan/advice scheme can provide flexibility for risky or new businesses. However those receiving loans may object to those getting grants and it may prove very difficult to determine criteria to separate these cases. In most cases, if a business is viable, it ought to be able to repay a loan.

b) The more complex the scheme, the more difficult it will be to carry on independently, under local auspices, as it will require higher managerial skills. Perhaps simple = self-sustainable?

c) The availability of loans can mean that the need for management or technical advice is overlooked by staff and applicants, in the details of the loan application.

d) It can be difficult to achieve self-financing, revolving loan funds. With relatively small loans the administration costs are high. Also, the loan fund capital is subject to the higher rates of inflation in poorer countries. But it can be shown that relatively high rates of interest to cover all programme costs make little difference to the repayments over the average 16 month repayment period, and make even less difference to the business viability. If you don't believe us, calculate the monthly repayments for a $100 loan at 10% and 20% interest!

e) Sometimes there are restrictions on charging interest to refugees, especially in Islamic countries or on giving the refugees any preferential rates to the local population.

f) It is necessary to have a hard-headed approach to loan repayments. Agencies' seen as being "soft options" usually fail.

g) Unless local staff are well trained, there can be difficulties in the assessment of business problems and in deciding on the right advice.

h) These schemes are usually run by specialist agencies, but need not be if planned carefully.

O. EMPLOYMENT BUREAU

O1. Employment Bureau Comments

Only one programme in our survey, in Pakistan, operated an employment bureau and this was closed, because it ceased to be acceptable to the host government for external reasons.

An employment bureau is clearly a way, and possibly a cost-effective way, of matching refugees to job opportunities. There are an enormous number of these organizations run by governments and private businesses, in nearly every country in the world. However, host countries are unlikely to allow employment bureaux for refugees to be set up, unless they are purely refugee jobs within refugee aid agencies, or the government is totally committed to refugees becoming fairly permanent inhabitants of their country. The situation has to be very stable for either type of bureau.

Employment bureaux for refugees are far more numerous in the richer countries. And there are also resettlement programmes to richer countries, which include help with finding employment in the new host country, learning English as a second language and also work/home skills, before the refugees leave their country of first asylum. One such programme is described in the handbooks "Shifting Gears", aimed at Cambodian refugees going to the USA; details can be found in the bibliography.

We have included employment bureaux in this book partly because they were mentioned by at least one respondent and partly because they are a highly valuable way of helping people find jobs in appropriate circumstances and countries. It is to be hoped that as refugees prove their worth in host countries and the employment opportunities in these countries improves, the employment bureaux will become a more common form of assistance.

FURTHER DETAILS (Sections P. to Z.)

P. POSSIBLE PROJECTS AND BUSINESSES - A LIST

The following list came from an analysis of the country programmes operated by 47 different organizations. The information came from questions A1., A2., A5. and A25. in the questionnaire analysis and from organizations which sent reports of their activities, instead of a completed questionnaire.

The use of the terms "activity", "business" and "project" should be clarified:- any independent action by an organization is an activity, so projects dealing with many different businesses or potential businesses have many activities, and projects dealing with just one type of business or even just one business have one activity. Here the number given in brackets after each item gives the number of organizations that mentioned that activity, e.g., Tailor (20) means 20 organizations are doing something in that field, not that 20 tailors are being helped by organizations - ACORD alone has helped at least 236 tailors.

We have only mentioned a given type of activity once, under one heading, but many could have been listed under more than one; it is to be hoped that this comprehensive list will provide some inspiration to readers of this book who are wondering what the refugees whom they are trying to assist can possibly do.

RELIEF SUBSTITUTION
Bedding - blankets (1), quilts (3)
Clothes (1), school uniforms (4)
School items - bags (2), chalk (1)
Tents (1)
Utensils (1)

ENVIRONMENT
Dams (1)
Erosion control (1)
Fuel-saving cookers (2)
Trees, Forestry (2)

INFRASTRUCTURE/CONSTRUCTION
Buildings (3) - e.g. clinics, offices, toilets.
Maintenance (3)
Roads (1)
Water supply (1), Irrigation (1)

BUSINESS STARTERS/INCOME-ADDING STARTERS/TRAINING SCHEMES

PRODUCTION	SERVICE	RETAIL
Metalwork (2)	Teashops (2)	"Blanket" stalls (2)
Blacksmith (6)	Restaurant (5)	Pushcart stalls (3)
Tinsmith (2)	Hotel (1)	"Kiosk" (1)
Tool-making (1)	Drink/Milk-selling (3)	Shops (2)
Bucket-making (1)	Water-selling (1)	Grocery (2)
Aluminium casting (1)	Donkey Cart (5)	General retail (4)
Welding (2)	Pick-up Truck (1)	Warehouse (1)
Soldering (1)	Driver (1)	Wholesale (1)
Tilly lamp making (1)	Car repair (5)	Marketing centres (2)
Turner (1)	Bodywork repair (3)	Woodsellers (2)
Wood furniture (9)	Car wheels/punctures (3)	Kerosene sellers (1)
Wood windows/doors (2)	Car-electric/charging (4)	Fishmonger (2)
Upholstery (1)	Car painting (2)	Second-hand clothing (2)
Tailoring (20)	Signmaking (3)	
Shoes/Cobblers (7)	Artwork (2)	

PRODUCTION	SERVICE	SERVICE
Charcoal (1) (6)	Screenprinting (1)	Radio/TV/watch repair
Building Lime (2)	Varnishing (1)	Sewing Machine repair (2)
Sisal/Rope (1)	Secretarial/Typing (3)	Electrical repair (5)
Mattress (2)	Accounts (1)	Motor rewiring (1)
Butchery (5)	Law office (1)	(Motor)Bicycle repair (3)
Bakery-bread (5)	Insurance office (1)	Photography (3)
Sweets (4)	Import/Export (1)	Henna Body painting (1)
Cakes (3)	Dentistry (1)	Clothes repair (2)
Local bread(nan, injera=3)	Nursing (1)	Shoe repair (2)
Jam (1)	Bookbinding (1)	Singing (1)
Ghee (1)	Dry cleaning (1)	Music Band (1)
Soft Drinks (3)	Laundry (1)	
Spagetti (1)	Waiters (1)	
Perfume (1)	Hairdressers/Barbers (5)	
Hair/facial cream (1)	Cereal grinding (2)	
Chocolate (1)	Cereal grinding machine repair (1)	
Soap (4)	Tool-sharpening (1)	
Stone cutting (2)	Masonry (3)	
Bricks (4)	Plumbers (2)	
Mud bricks (1)	House paintings (2)	
Clay bricks (1)	Well boring (1)	
Fuel brickettes (1)	Well digging (1)	
Handpumps (2)		
Handcarts (1)		
Donkey-carts (1)		

SMALL FARM PRODUCTION

Vegetable gardening (7)	Poultry (10)
Bees (3)	Sheep (2)
Dairy (2)	Pigs (1)
Camels (1)	

AGRICULTURE/FISHING

Group farms (8)	Cereals (1)
Fruit trees (1)	Fishing (3)

VILLAGE CRAFTS/HANDICRAFTS

Clay/Pottery - cookers(3)	Cotton beater (1)
- cooker repair (2)	Cotton carder (1)
- water jars (1)	Weaving (3)
- pots (3)	Spinning (1)
Incense maker (1)	Dyeing (1)
Baskets (2)	Tie-dyeing (2)
Mats (4)	Thread dyeing (1)
Rope (1)	Carpets (3)
Fishnet-making (1)	Embroidery (3)
Leatherwork (1)	Shawls (1)
Hats (3)	Knitting (1)
Ornaments/Decorations (1)	Machine knitting (1)
Jewellery-making (3)	

Q. QUESTIONS ON THE SELECTION OF PARTICIPANTS

Q1. Two Questions - Whom do you want to work with?
How do you choose participants?

A diverse range of people with different needs exists within any refugee population and many agencies target on particular groups. Or sometimes, the process of choosing objectives, geographical areas or a specific type of project determines the groups of people who will participate. A programme to help the poorest will, almost certainly, exclude some entrepreneurs. Choosing a camp in a rural area reduces some of the business options. Business starters often favour men as they are more likely to be looking for full-time jobs, and so special provisions need to be made for women.

Alternatively, if a specific grouping is the agency's focus this may well affect the type of income-generation project the agency implements and also the plans and methods for implementation.

Having set the objectives and the type of IG programme, there are still many questions concerning the choice of participants. Most programmes cover less than 1% of the total refugee population in their area and have waiting lists of some description. More refugees want some answer to "what now", than can join IG programmes.

In the following sections, we will deal first with the broader issues of participant selection, such as urban versus rural, and so on. One exception to this is the selection of women, which is covered in more detail in section S. Then, after these broader issues, we will examine actual procedures, showing how individual refugees are selected for the various types of programme.

Q2. Urban or Rural Origin?

The consensus of replies seems to suggest that urban refugees have more skills in income-generation. So urban refugees may be able to start more income-generating activities quicker than rural refugees. But there is often a significant group among the urban refugees, who have had an above average education and previously been employed as civil servants, teachers, administrators, or in other salaried positions. These people are often very difficult to assist through income-generating programmes or to place in other types of employment. This is because they either expect the same sort of employment, or they feel that their previous position would be demeaned if they took "lesser" jobs.

Rural refugees, where the land is available and similar to their homeland, can adapt quickly to some agriculture and other rural crafts, but only if the political conditions allow the use of that local land or resources.

Both urban and rural groups have such a wide range of backgrounds and skills that many different income-generating activities should be possible. The proportions may vary, but it is very bad planning to assume simple solutions, like agriculture for rural refugees and employment for urban refugees. It has often been suggested that in the initial registration questions on skills and experience would help greatly in planning future activities, not only income-generating, but for health, education, water supply and other services needed by the refugees.

Q3. Self-settled or in a Camp?

"Camps = Constraints" was a common feeling among respondents. Criticism covered the bureaucracy, logistical problems and the style of relief aid - though some camp refugees were felt to have better health, food and education, than non-camp refugees. It seems that the relief situation requires a large camp which is tightly controlled for efficiency. This is understandable to provide food, water and health supplies quickly. But large numbers of refugees in a small area make large demands on the local district (eg using fuel wood) and leave only a few resources available to be developed.

It is also difficult, in a camp, to develop the flexibility to allow an evolving range of activities. It is not impossible, but it does take longer to achieve the same sorts of objectives in a camp, than outside. It is also possible that in a large camp, a smaller proportion of the refugees can be assisted into business than in small camps or self-settled communities.

Those refugees who settle themselves, whether in rural areas, towns or cities, are thought to be better able to start IG activities, with or without assistance. Though they may have problems of discrimination or assimilation to overcome.

Q4. Entrepreneurs or the Poorest?

This is the subject of much discussion in the field of IG. It is always a dilemma: do you work with a small number of high-potential entrepreneurs or do you target the poorest and most needy members of the community? The entrepreneurs are likely to make better use of the assistance and perhaps employ others as well, but they are also likely to be the least needy and to have resources or at least skills already. The poorest people are those most obviously in need of help, and these forms of assistance are designed to help them, but the very fact of their poverty may mean they are busy trying to get resources simply to survive, and also may mean they are not very skilled or educated, even at basic levels.

In our survey twelve field workers commented specifically on these issues; for four of them, "work must be with the poorest" and they accepted the constraints of skill, education, and so on. The other eight said they worked with both groups and tried to include the poor, by techniques such as having a maximum loan size or working only in the poorest areas. They found the entrepreneurs in their programmes produced more tangible successes, which were valuable for employment and encouraged other refugees. In May 1987 a course for voluntary agencies interested in IG programmes (though not necessarily with refugees) was held at Cranfield School of Management. Half the thirty fieldworkers who attended chose the poorest, the other half chose entrepreneurs, when asked to decide which was more important. The debate following this question produced a much wider range of answers, not necessarily exclusive to either entrepreneurs or to the poorest.

If an agency works mostly with entrepreneurs, they tend to produce more "successful" programmes in quantifiable terms which usually need less continuing intervention from the agency. Many agencies have social as well as economic goals, such as working with the most disadvantaged. If this is the case, particular consideration needs to be given to such factors as criteria for participation, access to the programme, and the types of special assistance needed.

Refugee entrepreneurs, according to our business survey are likely to employ one family member and one other person besides themselves. But women refugee entrepreneurs are only likely to employ half these extra people. It is widely accepted that women very often get a raw deal as far as access to resources are concerned, and often those households without adult males are amongst the poorest. This is particularly critical in refugee situations where women and children can make up the majority of the population. Therefore, many agencies put the participation of women as a priority in the programme. Indeed, it is very important that such disadvantaged groups receive the assistance they need, even if it means excluding apparently high-potential entrepreneurs and concentrating on people who need more resources for apparently similar results.

Q5. The Disabled

Because many refugee communities have suffered from warfare, or other physical hardships, there are likely to be more disabled in these communities. Even if the numbers are normal, the disabled often have particular difficulties in participating in programmes which do not take into account their special needs.

Of the 149 programmes covered in our survey, two had special programmes for the handicapped. In the detailed replies to our survey from 15 organiizations, only 3 out of an average 638 refugees were handicapped. This is a low provision, and each programme should include some thought on making projects more accessible to handicapped or disabled refugees. No comments were given on how to do this, but the Ockenden Venture, in Port Sudan, set up a training centre for the severely disabled, initially in silk screen printing. This showed that such programmes need to provide a substantial amount of continuing support and assistance, over a long period; nevertheless, the refugees are gradually coming to the point where they can take over and manage the business themselves. Other handicapped people in programmes are not so lucky and cannot start their own business, because all the equipment is in the special workshop and there is no provision for loans or extension of the programme

Q6. I.G. for other Disadvantaged Groups

In some areas, membership of particular groups (such as "outcast" tribes, or small religious sects) means that people are excluded from general society and many of its resources. This can be particularly hard for those who have already been displaced. Where agencies have identified particular needy groups as having a priority, there seem to be two broad approaches:

1. To include them in a programme for the general population, but making some provision for any special needs they may have.
2. To plan special programmmes exclusively for them. These apply to the disabled as well as the disadvantaged.

The first approach has the advantage of not further excluding people from the rest of the population, however there is the danger of not planning sufficiently for particular needs. The second approach enables the agency to cater specifically for special needs, though there is the danger of a paternalistic approach which results in perpetuating dependency. The comments above on the handicapped, or in section S3. on women, may help decisions with regard to any disadvantaged group.

Q7. How do you choose the Participants?

Deciding the criteria for selection is largely determined by the target group(s) focused on by the agency, and whether the agency has social as well as economic objectives. Criteria may include:

a) <u>Wealth</u>: Those whose wealth exceeds a certain amount may be excluded. This may be defined in terms of capital, income, housing status or in other ways. The problem with this is that it can be almost impossible to find out the true wealth of an applicant unless, like ACORD, a logbook of all relevant information is built up and cross-checked. Moreover, deciding criteria for defining "wealth" can be very problematic and value-laden. For instance, a nomadic family living in a refugee camp may appear poverty stricken in their lifestyle to a foreigner, but they may have built up a sizeable herd of animals outside the camp. On the other hand, a town family in the same camp may appear to have more material possessions and yet have no security at all.

b) <u>Evidence of entrepreneurial skill</u>: They may, for instance, be able to demonstrate this by having started a business which has potential but needs some extra input. Of 15 organizations in our survey, only 15% of refugee businessmen/women had already started an enterprise in the host country and could therefore show this evidence. However, 72% of the business people were starting the same businesses in the host country as they had run previously. So most agencies had to rely on the word of the refugee or did some simple verbal or practical test.

We did not find any special entrepreneur "tests", which are often used by agencies, in poorer countries with the local population.

One informal method of testing entrepreneurship, is to ask applicants to carry out simple tasks, such as identifying sources of supplies, or finding out about competitive prices, or carrying out basic market surveys. This not only provides information, but, more importantly, tests whether the refugees are really willing to start a business.

c) <u>Evidence of business viability</u>: Another form of test is a study of the viability of the proposed business.

Business assistance programmes usually include a full study as part of their assistance, or they keep a detailed log book, as did the field workers in ACORD in Port Sudan.

Business starter programmes include long questionnaires, as in the AICF and ARC case studies, or a simple analysis form, like the one in section U. on loans, which came from the Quaker case study. Or sometimes each project may plan for a "break-even point", like the UNHCR test for handicraft production mentioned in section K3.

Income-adding starter programmes often look only at the programme viability (sometimes not even that!) and not the viability of the individual refugee activity. These omissions and possibly the lack of market surveys, may perhaps be understood as being an oversight on the part of staff anxious to do something. However, such studies may be irrelevant or a waste of time in very changing circumstances and it may be far better to make some personal assessment of the commitment and ability of the refugee.

d) <u>Ability to provide some guarantee</u>: A guarantee of some type is an advantage for those agencies making loans available. About half those agencies assisting businesses, gave loans, the others gave grants. More details of loans and guarantees are given in section U.

e) <u>Self selection</u>: The refugee comes to the agency - usually this is on a first come first served basis and it shows motivation. The agency then further selects by some limitation on the assistance available (e.g. loan/grant ceiling). This type of programme helps those that help themselves, but might miss some needy people, who would have greatly benefitted from the assistance, but missed their chance because they did not hear about the scheme in time.

f) <u>A quota system</u>: One or two respondents had programmes allocating a certain number of places in the programme to specifically defined groups of people, such as the disabled. Though no figures are available, this did not seem to be used often, possibly because of the clumsiness of operation - cross-checking is needed for every applicant to see if they fulfil the particular criteria.

Q8. How do you gain access to those you want to work with?

As soon as any IG programme is announced, there is usually a flood of enquiries and calls for assistance, and often these include requests, which cannot be fulfilled by that programme. However, the agency may want to help specific groups of people other than those who take the first step in approaching the office or the workers. Possible ways of overcoming this may include:

a) Making provision in the programme to meet the special needs of particular groups. For instance, if the participation of women is a priority, an understanding of the women's lifestyle is important, before deciding on special arrangements to help the women apply.

A common observation, by outsiders, of male refugees, is that they spend large amounts of their time idle, totally displaced from their usual work patterns. In comparison, women refugees continue to be responsible for children, washing, cooking, collecting firewood.

Activities which increase the womens' income are often an extension of their chores or on a part time basis, fitted in between the chores. Thus the criteria for participation and management advice need to take this into account, by meeting women in places or at times convenient for them, by trying to reduce their domestic work load, and by designing loans, repayments or whatever other assistance conditions exist, to fit part-time work.

Similarly for other special groups, an understanding of the people must come before designing and implementing a programme.

b) Organizing for outreach work. Since the neediest people may not get information through official channels, like notice boards or meetings, and they might not even hear through the informal channels, like word of mouth, then reaching out to possible participants may have to be done by the agency. The old, the handicapped, the sick, the women who cannot move freely outside for cultural reasons, the poor who are very busy trying to get enough to eat - all these groups can be missed by programmes that are only centre-based or that rely on other refugees to spread the word about them.

Individual contact of this kind may appear expensive, but it may be necessary to supplement or even to replace the existing methods, should it be suspected that significant groups of people are not being served by the programme. If careful consideration is given to how this should be done, it can be effective, for example, the GTZ programme going out to sell their fuel-saving cookers shown in section I4.

R. THE REFUGEES' VIEWPOINT

R1. Not a Study from the Refugees' Perspective

Looking at informal figures from Pakistan, Somalia and Sudan, about 30% of refugees go straight into local towns and cities and do not usually get any assistance. A further 10% may seek assistance for allowances, training or resettlement in those towns and cities - these tend to be the more educated of the refugee population.

Our study concentrated on agency assistance, with only one of the three questionnaires concentrating on points from the refugees' perspective. But we did ask the field workers to try and find refugee businesses, both those they had assisted and those that received no assistance. Both were given the same business questionnaire. 24 out of the 124 refugee businesses questioned had received no assistance, but surprisingly there were no significant differences. Even the starting capital needed was the same, though one might have expected agencies to give more and perhaps that refugees would have tried to ask for more from "these rich expatriates".

It must be remembered that businesses in relatively developed areas, such as capital cities, need much more starting capital and the refugees there are likely to be more educated and looking for higher levels of capital. However, the capital given by agencies and the capital found by non-assisted refugees in these areas seems comparable. Much more work could be done researching these "self-starter" refugees, checking these results and seeing if there are lessons for providing assistance, since there were no significant differences between the self-starter and assisted refugees in the business survey.

R2. Agencies and Refugee Perspectives

The agencies felt that refugees were more concerned about reliable sources of money (4 replies) and inadequate supplies (2 replies), than about management. One reply stated that "family and life come before business".

The following table summarizes the problems as the refugees themselves saw them when they started their businesses, and the problems they face now and the help they would like from agencies or governments.

TABLE 7. Business Problems and Assistance - as seen by refugees

STARTING PROBLEMS		PRESENT PROBLEMS		HELP WANTED NOW	
Getting money	75%	Getting money	33%	Getting a loan	57%
Getting supplies	35%	Low sales	31%	More customers	38%
Low sales	32%	Competition	25%	Skill training	30%
Poor selling place	21%	Poor selling place	20%	A new site	22%
Tools/machines	20%	Tools/machines	19%	Accounting training	10%
Competition	15%	Getting supplies	16%	Laws/taxes/etc	6%
Low skills	12%	Transport	8%		
Transport	7%	(All others were under 5% - see questions C.22,23,25)			

These seem to indicate that the agencies have some understanding of the refugees' real concerns; though only 3% of refugees felt record-keeping was a problem - much less than agencies' efforts to get proper accounts would suggest.

R3. Other Comments

The two "average" refugee case studies also show other data on refugee business finance, family, workers and the future, for Sudan and Pakistan, but readers should refer to Questionnaire C. for details elsewhere.

S. WOMEN REFUGEES IN INCOME-GENERATING PROJECTS

S1. Introduction
It is unfortunately true that the majority of IG projects, except handicraft ones, do not help women. In many programmes, those responsible are not even aware of the extent of this failure, since no data is collected about the women. In the evaluation section Y we suggest that all projects should record the numbers of women they assist, and encourage the more active involvement of women.

Women refugees have the triple disadvantage of being in poor countries, being refugees, and having the disadvantages imposed on women. Summarising these briefly, as they affect IG projects, these disadvantages are:

In poor countries	- lack of jobs - low purchasing power - marketing problems - supply problems
For refugees	- new environment (markets, contacts, language) - restrictions on licenses, ownership, travel, etc
For women	- usually household obligations (so work is part-time and local) - lack of education or training - the traditional position of women (at home, family role first, restrictions on certain jobs)

S2. Statistics
In eleven projects (not including the next four) with an average of 632 participants each, 44 were women in all-women businesses (7%) and 88 women were included in businesses with men (14%), a total of 21% women.

In four handicraft and relief substitution projects, the proportion was reversed, the average was 86% women.

In the refugee business survey, 27% of the businesses were owned by women. It was difficult to generalize about figures as each country was different, but the following were consistent trends:

a) The capital to start is lower (on average 60% of men's), it often comes from the family and is rarely borrowed.
b) Women earn a lower income, though it is very variable depending on the type of business.
c) Their skills are more likely to be acquired from their family or their own previous business. They were most unlikely to have been trained or to have worked for others.
d) Their businesses are about half as likely to employ others (compared to men's businesses).
e) Women's businesses are more likely to remain local - very few thought of expanding beyond their present business site.
f) Women seem to work better in groups than men.
f) Women are a better risk for loans - they are more likely to repay.
g) Unless desperate (widowed, single parents), more women in business are either young or old (before and after child rearing), than the equivalent business age distribution of men. In fact most women in projects are the older more experienced ones - there is some evidence that young women, who have missed out on education, are the forgotten people in IG projects.

S3. But what to do? Separate Projects or Special Conditions?
There is no doubt that women are given less assistance, but how should agencies compensate for these disadvantages? As with other special groups, one way is to have special projects only for women and another way is to ensure the women receive a proper share of assistance, by special conditions within a general project.

Many people support special projects for women, because they deal specifically with problems like lack of education, and inability to travel, whereas general projects often contain these as "hidden" conditions that are biased against women.

In projects for both men and women, which actively assist the women, arguments occur - why should special resources go to them, what about the handicapped and other disadvantaged? This produces a situation where women are viewed as a discriminated against, disadvantaged minority and not a valuable resource. Both these styles of project seem to put women into a "minority" or a "disadvantaged" category, rather than the majority they are. So we would argue that these may be the wrong starting points and instead it is important to look at all the opportunities and try to produce programmes which match the refugee population and the conditions within that population.

Separate projects may be permissable if the assistance cannot be given to both sexes at the same time or in the same way. For example, either sex can do vegetable gardening, but it may be that the refugees need training, and that the women cannot be trained with the men, because the women sit at the back and do not ask questions. Or the women must garden in groups, because their family responsibilities mean they cannot work full-time. A womens gardening project was created for just these reasons by the Quakers.

However, most business programmes work with individuals and with a range of assistance and there is no reason for separate projects. Indeed, if the programme is properly targetted at the poorest, there should be more women than men participants, as women outnumber men and they are poorer. Even from a business only perspective, the women repay loans better, so they should form a higher percentage of those assisted. But how should an IG programme work properly? The following might help:

1. Equal numbers of male and female staff should be employed at all levels - if the women are worse educated, they should receive more training.
2. Equal access - in camps, placing a service near the camp administration attracts mostly men and placing it near a primary health centre attracts mostly women. In towns, placing an office in the centre discriminates against women, as they spend their lives more locally. The district centres started by ACORD overcame this problem. Careful consideration is needed in choosing a good base, or for outreach work, if a good base is not available.
3. Equal publicity - publicise not only through refugee adminstrations, teashops or other places men meet, but the women's informal networks should also be used.
4. Equal funds should be available - as women are likely to use less capital, on a more short-term basis. Equal funds should be in two or more categories, for example the hire purchase, short-term loans and microcredit of ACORD. But each category should be open to men and women.

The starting points, in each case, are the opportunities, not the gender and this gets away from the issue of women being a "minority". To create projects just for women, which exclude the men, is just as bad as designing with inherent "hidden" conditions for men. It is in the planning stage for those opportunities that it is appropriate to consider all the refugee population, both men and women.

T. FIRST STEPS IN MARKETING

T1. Introduction

Markets have already been mentioned in several sections, since they are so fundamental to IG activities. Marketing is covered by many simple handbooks, and they are mostly applicable to refugees, though refugees may be new to these markets and their legal position is less clear.

It is remarkable, how often basic points of marketing are missed, so any refugee thinking of entering business and certainly any agency giving assistance to businesses, should both ask and answer all the following questions to their own satisfaction, before starting.

T2. The Customers

Who will buy my product or service?
Why will they buy it?
How will they know about it?
How will the product or service reach them?

T3. The Right Product or Service

What is needed?
What is wanted?
What are customers willing and able to pay?
Where must the product or service be provided?

T4. The Right Quality

What goods or services are already on the market?
How will my product or service be better?
What is the price for what quality?
What comments do customers make on the use, price and quality?
How can the product or service be improved in quality, price,
reliability, delivery or to suit other requirements of the customers?

T5. The Right Quantity

How quickly will the goods be sold or how often the service used? (Ask others)
Is the demand seasonal or it is steady through out the year?
How quickly can the product be restocked or how long does the service take?
Any special characteristics of this product or service:
- Is transportation difficult?
- Can it perish or go out of fashion?
- Is it likely to suffer from <u>sudden</u> new supplies or shortages or new competition?
- Is it large or difficult to store?
- Anything else?

How quickly can you change the speed of production or service to match changes in demand or changes in supply?

T6. The Right Price (and Profit?)

What is the cost to you? (Include all costs, labour, transport, rents, and a reasonable profit or earnings)
How will the costs be affected by such changes as in T5.?
What is the price in the market? (For the same, better or worse quality)
What are the competitors doing? (Are the prices going up or down? Why?
And look for unsold goods - a sign of market saturation)

T7. Improving the Business

Are there more potential markets - different people or further away?
Are there marketing organisations (public or private) to help?
Is the most time spent on the things that make the most money?
Would lowering prices, increase sales?
Would increasing prices and quality, increase sales?
Would more people buy, if there was credit available?
Is notice taken of customers comments?
Can the service be improved?
Could the product or service be advertised better?
- Better layout or notices, posters, signs, word of mouth, loudspeaker or radio. Do important people use the product or service - could you use this fact?

Is there overstocking or a waste of materials?
Could alternatives be used?
Can the costs of transport or credit be reduced?
Could a group of you, doing the same thing, share costs or resources?
Can anything be done to reduce other costs - rents, staff, bulk buying, etc?

T8. The Right Channels (Certain businesses only)

What shops, distributers, vendors or other selling channels may be needed?
Do these channels exist already, or will you create them?
What differences do these channels make to costs and prices (e.g. discounts or paying for the distribution)?

U. LOANS AND GUARANTEES

U1. Introduction

About half of IG agencies give grants (or equipment), and half provide loans. But when the word business is used in the name of the IG scheme, the proportion providing loans goes to over 90%. Perhaps, in business, grants are not acceptable, it is no longer charity and subsidies are frowned upon. With IG programmes, the distinction between aid and business is blurred and whatever the truth, many agencies, working with poor people, refugees or not, have had problems with loans:

> If a disaster occurs - like a crop failure with agricultural loans, should agencies insist on taking the poor person's guarantee, their land and tools, and leave them worse off than before the loan?

> If a borrower defaults - do you put a person, especially a refugee in jail? Having already left one country, for more freedom, this may seem unduly unfair and paradoxical.

> If the business fails - is it the agencies' fault for funding a failure or is he or she bad at business? And who pays?

> If there is no penalty - what is to stop a refugee from spending the money or selling the equipment? But a refugee has very little to guarantee a loan, so what security is possible?

U2. Statistics

In the survey of 124 refugee businesses, we can divide them into three groups:

Group 1. 65 received a loan as their main assistance (7 of them also had a grant)
         20 received cash only
         20 were given equipment only, which they then repaid the value in cash
         25 received a combination loan of cash and equipment
(Most businesses also received advice)

Group 2. 33 received a grant of equipment
         (4 also received a cash grant)

Group 3. 26 received no material assistance from an agency
         (2 of these did receive some advice or training)

However, this is too simple a view of refugee businesses. Many refugees, assisted or not, obtained cash or equipment for their businesses from many sources:

TABLE 8. How refugees assist their own businesses.

Source of Cash/ Equipment	No. in Group 1 (loans)	No. in Group 2 (grants)	No. in Group 3 (no assistance)	% Total
Cash from Home	7	13	10	24
Gift from Family/Ref.s/Locals	4	6	3	10
Borrowed from Famil/Ref.s/Locals	9	12	7	23
Saved while a refugee	25	7	9	33
Brought Equipment from Home	12	1	9	18

The figures in Table 8. are slightly different from those in the Appendix, because of the "any other answer" category, but the overwhelming conclusion is that these refugees are trying hard to start a business. Especially those receiving loans - they were working hard to save some capital, before they had a loan.

Further points:

- Some that received loans from agencies also borrowed money elsewhere.
- A third of those receiving grants also borrow, but not from the agency.
- Only a quarter of those that received no assistance borrow money; their main starting capital or equipment was brought with them.

There seems little difference between the three groups when it comes to the amount of the starting capital. The differences are between men and women and between industrialized and rural economies.

In the rural areas of poor countries and in their small towns with similar businesses, the starting capital average was less than $300 per person. For Somalia and Pakistan, the average was $170.

In richer countries, such as the West Bank, or in capital cities, like Nairobi, and towns with high rents, various amenities, and other indicators of a complex, rather than a village economy, the average starting capital is likely to be between $1,000 to $10,000, depending on the country and circumstances.

The range of loans for both rich and poor groups was 10-200% of the average loan. The repayment was usually done on a monthly basis (with some seasonal adjustment if necessary) over a 16 month period.

The agencies estimated that 18% of the refugees were in arrears and 10% would default. For four programmes, annual interest was 13%, 5% and free for the other two.

Access to money for business (usually loans) is important to refugees, as was shown in section R. - 75% gave it as a starting problem, 33% as a continuing problem and 57% would like a loan.

U3. What are the Issues to Think about?

A great deal has been written about promoting enterprises in developing countries, and much of it also applies to refugee assistance programmes. These sources cover most of the issues of loans and credit and it is very difficult to do justice to them all here. We refer to one source in particular, "A Manual for Savings and Credit for the Poor of Developing Countries" (Oxfam 1987). Most of it does apply to refugees, but not all.

In the following sections we will use the same order of topics used in the Oxfam book, summarizing and adding comments from our own experience and research on refugees and loans.

U4. The Refugee Economy

Like the families in rural areas of poor countries, the business element of refugee families is integrated with the general family economy and it is almost impossible to separate them. This means that business is fitted into the other family, household and social obligations. Investment in business has to be weighed not against simple economic criteria, but against all the other uses of that money. Similarly, credit is seen in the same way - not necessarily to be used exclusively for the business, but as part of the family resources. Hence many agencies do not loan money, they loan equipment, which is then repaid in cash. Even some of those agencies giving grants, do not give money - they give equipment, as do ARC and AICF in Pakistan.

There is a counter argument that says this is paternalistic, not allowing refugees to be responsible for money and in the Quaker case study, cash was lent for this reason, with three definite cases from 51 businesses of "abuse" (we would prefer "divertion") of the money into family obligations.

U5. The Need for Credit and Access to Credit

The refugees' need for credit is even higher than that of local people, which is in itself high in developing countries (20% per month is not uncommon in informal lending). And their access to credit seems lower than for corresponding local people. Often the agency is the only source of credit available, besides the family. This situation arises initially as refugees lack contacts and resources. As time goes on, other sources of credit, like money lenders or shop credit do become available to refugees in ways similar to local people.

This pattern of refugees being similar to local people, but more extreme, is true in many aspects. Local people need credit and access to credit; refugees have even less. Local people make a high proportion of their livelihood in the subsistence, not cash, economy. The refugees come with very little money, and with free relief goods, they are even further removed from a cash economy. So it takes a while for a cash economy to develop. The small amount of money initially brought with them, is supplemented by jobs in health, education and construction and sales of rations. All these bring in money to start the refugee cash economy (unless it is "Food-for-Work").

In saying refugees sometimes sell part of their rations, we do not wish to suggest that there is an oversupply of rations. Rather, the quantities of rations consist of a very few basic items and in order to buy other items or to save to start a small enterprise some may be sacrificed.

U6. Guarantees and Security for the Loans

As we have already suggested the issues of guarantees and the security of loans is a very difficult one for refugees. Of 8 organizations replying to this question:

   5 use a written contract (See ACROSS and Quaker examples)
   3 used collateral, usually the equipment provided.
   1 used a Ration Book pass number
   1 used a Loan Committee (ACROSS with both refugees and locals)
   1 used group security (ACORD- but two other organisations mentioned this in their thinking)
   1 needed no security - the staff are present at the handover and said "they [the refugees] know us" (see AICF Case study).

Many development agencies in poor countries do not themselves lend money to small-scale business people, but they operate guarantee schemes for lenders, usually commercial banks. If borrowers default, the agency pays the bank perhaps 80% or even more of the sum lost. We only found two examples of this with refugees, SPAREK in Nairobi, Kenya and PFP in Somalia (this project has now ended). This type of guarantee extends the number of people that agencies can help, without extending the money needed.

It seems that the closer the agencies are to the refugees and their traditional structures, the less written contracts are needed or the less formal and legal the contracts need to be, though the threat of taking back equipment is used verbally. This closeness can be achieved by involving traditional leaders, or sometimes the administrative leaders, if they are well respected or have close control in the community. Alternatively, regular discussions between the agency staff and the refugee builds up trust as they work together to produce a good proposal. The Analysis Form, on the next page, was used by the Quakers in Somalia and did just this - it often took several drafts to get the figures right and work out the loans and repayments. The form was the originally in Somali and shows the proposal for Hassan's stone-cutting group (see the case studies of refugee businesses).

Group security perhaps needs more explanation and an example may help: five individuals, who are not related, each want to be given loans. The first one gets the loan, and not until this loan or a proportion of it is repaid does the next get a loan, and so on. Each is still individually liable, but there is group pressure to repay. This has worked extremely well with small loans of under $300. We have no examples using this system with big loans for refugees, although it has been widely applied in different forms to non-refugees in poor areas.

We found no examples of credit unions (where people save together and then loan the amount to one of the savers) with refugees - possibly because of the lack of cash in the refugee economy. Though such unions may evolve in the future.

U7. Agreement Forms

We include here two examples of agreement forms, from the Quakers in Somalia and from ACROSS in Sudan. The Quaker form has very simple conditions and uses a guarantee of collateral, the equipment, a guarantor or a combination. The ACROSS form is more complete and includes other systems readers may wish to use.

Quaker Programme

SMALL BUSINESS MONTHLY ANALYSIS FORM   Name: Hassan   Section: 12

LOAN (Capital Costs)				OWN EQUIPMENT			
Item	Price	No.	Total	Item	Price	No.	Total
Crowbar	600	3	1,800	Crowbar	600	1	600
Spades	200	4	800	Spades	200	2	200
Hammers	300	4	1,200	Pickaxes	300	4	1,200
Chisels	200	4	800				

(The "Capital Costs" mean those purchases, which are not consumed each month)

(This quarter is useful to see what the refugees are contributing, but is not used in the calculations)

TOTAL   5,800

LOAN (Running Costs)				INCOME PER MONTH			
Item	Price	No.	Total	Item	Price	No.	Total
Sack Rice	400	1	400	Load	600	15	9,000
Sack Sugar	450	1	450				
Tea/kg	55	4	220				

(The "Running Costs" mean regular monthly recurring costs - here a simple lunch and drink)

(The six men cut a lorry load of stones every two days)

TOTAL   1,070   TOTAL   9,000

TOTAL LOAN NEEDED =   6,870

LOAN PERIOD = 12 MONTHS

THEREFORE MONTHLY REPAYMENT = 575

INCOME - RUNNING COSTS - MONTHLY REPAYMENT = MONTHLY PROFIT

9,000 - 1,070 - 575 = 7,355

NOTE 1. - There is no interest, no depreciation and no savings, but the plan was for them to save the repayment amount, once the loan was repaid.

NOTE 2. - All figures are in Somali Shillins - 1,000 Sh per month was an average wage (about $60), these six men hoped to get 1,225 per month. All the figures were checked with local prices - but no-one planned on an eighteen month drought. Turn back to Hassans story on p.45.

Quaker Programme

SMALL BUSINESS LOAN AGREEMENT FORM

Business Name _____

Loan Amount	_____	Somali Shillings
Monthly Repayment	_____	Somali Shillings
Date Repayments Start	_____	(2 months after loan made)
Date Repayments End	_____	(Less than 12 months after start)

RULES
1. The loan should only be used for the business.
2. The loan is only for the named people.
3. The participants must meet the business advisor regularly.
4. The participants must tell the advisor any business or repayment problems. The advisor will try to reach an agreement with the participants on how to deal with the problems.
5. The repayments are to made into the Small Business Account at the local bank each month.

GUARANTEE
The participants guarantee the loan with the following:

	Item	Cost
Project items, which can be resold	_____	____
	_____	____
	_____	____
Personal goods, which can be sold	_____	____
	_____	____
	_____	____
Name of a Guarantor: _____	_____	____

The total must add up to the total loan   TOTAL = _____

If the repayments are not made and an agreement is not made, then the Camp Administration, the Police and the Courts may be involved to claim the guarantee.

NAMES (Signatures)_____

_____

ADDRESSES _____

_____

Signature for the Quakers _____

Signature for the Camp Administration _____

Date _____

(In five copies for Refugees, Quakers, Administration, Police and Court)

ACROSS Programme

- MARIDI COMMUNIY DEVELOPMENT DEPARTMENT
LOAN CONTRACT

File_____   Date_____

A. BORROWER INFORMATION
1) Name:
2) If a Society, Name of Chairman:
3) Location of Borrowers Home:
4) If Borrower has a Business, Location of Business:
5) Purpose of Loan:
6) Has this Client had Previous Loans from ACROSS?
   If Yes, List Date Previous Loan was repaid in full, or
   Amount still outstanding:

B. DETAILS OF LOAN

1) Cash Issued by ACROSS to Borrower   Total £S
   In Words:
2) Materials Issued by ACROSS to Borrower   Total £S
   In Words:

3) Total Value of Loan Issued   Total £S
   In Words:

C. TERMS OF REPAYMENT
1) Total Time Allowed for Loan Repayment
2) Installments to be paid: Monthly Quarterly Semi-annually Other
3) Date first Installment is due:
4) Dates of Subsequent Installments:
5) Number of Installments to be paid:
6) Date Final Installment is due:
7) Administrative fee: % of Total Loan Value per year
8) Amount of Each Installment Payment:
   Principal   + Admin Fee   = Total

9) Total to be repaid £S
In Words:

D. SECURITY

Either 1) Describe Goods being pledged as Collateral to Guarantee this Loan and state their Value:

Or 2) Signature of Person Guaranteeing this Loan in Event Borrower
is Unable to Repay it:
Name:
Position:

E. OTHER SPECIAL TERMS OR INSTRUCTIONS:

F. CONDITIONS OF LOAN
I, the borrower, accept the following conditions for this loan:

1) I agree to repay the loan on schedule with the listed terms.

2) If I cannot make a payment on schedule, I will immediately notify ACROSS Community Development Department.

3) I will make up late payments as soon as possible.

4) ACROSS CD Department reserves the right to charge a late payment penalty in cases of unexcused non-payment, according to the agreed schedule.

5) If I fail to make payments on time, and if I fail to notify ACROSS CD Department of that, and I do not try to catch up with the payment schedule, ACROSS has the right to repossess my cash or goods. ACROSS also has the right to take legal action to recover its investment.

6) ACROSS CD Department has the right to add to my account the value of small items I order from them. A new loan agreement will not be necessary. My monthly payment amount will not increase, but I will pay for a longer time. These records will be kept in a cash book.

7) I agree to keep accurate business records. I will make reports to ACROSS CD Department, when requested.

8) If I participate in any illegal or dishonest business activity, or if I violate the terms of this contract, ACROSS has the right to demand immediate repayment of the balance of my loan. If I do not pay as ordered, ACROSS can repossess my goods or start legal action.

Signature of CD Advisor   Date

Signature of Borrowers   Date

Signature Of Lender   Date

Three copies to Borrower, ACROSS CD Department, CD Advisor in Settlement

U8. Default

Businesses do fail or falter for many reasons. Is it fair to penalise the business man or woman? As we suggested earlier, it is particularly difficult to deal with defaulters when they are refugees.

Although the Quakers in Somalia did ask the police to catch two defaulters, (who were actually never found), most agencies in our survey, including the Quakers, do not like the idea of imprisoning refugees and use it as a last resort.

Usually on default the equipment is returned, but any cash outstanding is written off. Fortunately, in most cases the equipment is relatively valuable compared to the cash loan and other refugees are not tempted by this concession to default.

Because of the careful design of the projects, the choice of businesses, the guarantees and the often close and continuous attention, average refugee loan projects have only a 10% default rate. Banks in richer countries usually see 10% default as very bad, whilst many lenders in poor countries regard it as quite good, since 35% defaults, or even higher is common.

U9. Repayment

All the evidence shows that the smaller the loan, the better the chances of repayment - especially if the borrowers are women. Nevertheless, because of seasonal factors, the unreliability of supplies, and many other factors, an average of eighteen per cent of borrowers do get into arrears. A combination of early detection and immediate discussions leading to agreed rescheduling of debts seems to work. Leaving the situation to see if it gets better usually means it gets worse.

Simple, current and on-the-spot record keeping for the loan programme itself is vital. Systems which rely on centralised, slow record keeping, are likely to lead to arrears. Computers, which rely on slow human inputs and even slower human analysis, will give the arrears figures very accurately, but not very usefully.

U10. Interest

Most refugees assume that the aid agencies are "very, very rich - (even if they are not)" and the refugees can see for themselves the big cars, big houses and smart clothes of the agency staff. So it is not surprising that some refugees assume the loan is really a grant for "why do they need the money?"

So, should interest be charged to show the seriousness of the loan and how it increases if they default? No, this does not seem to reduce the number of defaulters - in many countries, where some borrowers continue to believe either that the agency does not need the money or that the money is actually theirs, since it was "given" to help them.

Loans are more often repaid when the refugees can see where the money goes or can trust those administering the money. This seems to be a function of "closeness" - the nearer the agency is to the refugees, the more likely the repayment. The level of interest rates seems to play a minor role in repayment. Small short-term loans at 1% a day (or 365% a year!) are quite common and when asked, the borrowers wondered how the <u>agency</u> made any money!

So, if interest rates are not very important to the refugees, to whom are they important and why? In the early stages after the relief phase, the agencies are used to giving money with no "returns", and the refugees are used to that style. A sudden jolt into being asked for payment is too difficult for the agencies to implement.

At the other end of the scale, near flexible development, agencies need the interest to try to make their programmes self-sustainable and they need any income they can get to cover the costs of:

    Administration
    Inflation
    Default and even
    Expansion?

We did not find any loan schemes with refugees that came near the goal of self-sustainability; there is always an element of subsidy. However, ACORD came closest and the closer an agency comes to covering its costs, the more possible becomes the dream of truly independent agencies.

U11. Credit is Not Enough

Very simply, it is most unlikely that credit is the only problem a business has. Credit should be part of an integrated sytem of support which helps the businesses.

Paradoxically, it would seem that any other single form of assistance, like grants, would also not be enough. But the toolkits given by AICF and ARC in Pakistan, were not accompanied by any other assistance and they produced success rates of about 80-90%. Similar rates of success came from the loan schemes of the Quakers and ACORD. Obviously, the successful IG project is not based on grants or loans alone, but on the types and timing of assistance and how it is given.

If a scheme only provides credit, it will fail to assist those businesses that need other help and it may well provide more credit than is necessary. It is not enough to offer credit; look at the other assistance that is needed as well.

V. NON-FINANCIAL ASSISTANCE

V1. Introduction

We have just suggested (in U11.) that loans and grants are not enough to help businesses, what else can be offered to existing or prospective business people? Leaving out skills training which is covered in other sections, there are many possibilities. We received replies from seventeen organizations, to question A.29, on the possibilities for non-financial assistance.

V2. Feasibility Studies or Business Plans (Before Starting)

Three agencies mentioned that they produced or demanded comprehensive business plans before they assisted any business. One agency said this was only done informally on visits. As suggested before, it could be that more attention should be given to this form of assistance - perhaps a more systematic approach is needed to look at the viability of all projects.

V3. Business Counselling (after Starting)

Similar to V2., three agencies said they provided regular business counselling for all "their" businesses; and two further agencies gave some counselling informally on visits. Perhaps it needs specialist agencies to be able to understand business problems and advise on solutions?

V4. Business Training Courses (Before and After Starting)

Two organizations provided management courses for all their participants and one other trained half the business people they assisted, most of whom were just starting their enterprises. It is normal that existing businesses seem to have a higher rate of success than "start-ups", but the difference is not so pronounced with refugees, perhaps because all the enterprises are relatively new and precarious.

One organization ran a special course for illiterate refugee business people.

V5. Production Assistance

    a) With raw materials - 4 agencies gave to all participants (all handicraft programmes) and 4 gave material to some businesses.
    b) With production/vocational training - (though not as a main objective) 1 agency trained all participants, 6 did some training.
    c) Individual advice - 4 agencies advised all participants, 4 some.
    d) Machinery supply - 2 agencies supplied for most participants, 3 some.
    e) Other - One agency helped with production control, another with quality control.

In general most agencies are involved with some sort of production or technical assistance.

V6. License or Regulations Assistance

Two organizations mentioned this in the Sudan, but with little success. Perhaps many agencies also obtain licences or give assistance in conforming to local regulations, but have not seen this as a separate form of assistance, or perhaps there is more potential for this type of assistance.

V7. Marketing Assistance

a) Through introductions or contacts - 3 agencies for all participants, 2 for some.
b) Through the agencies' own buying power - 2 agencies bought all the refugee production, 2 bought some, 3 just small numbers.
c) Other - 2 agencies assisted production to get to other outlets or organizations, 1 assisted export, 1 did a market survey, 1 gave advice.

V8. Other Forms of Assistance

One agency gave technical advice and one literacy training.

V9. Concluding Comments on Non-Financial Assistance

Though much of this assistance is informal and cannot easily be categorised or described, it cannot be over-emphasised that without these smaller inputs, some of the grants or loans provided by agencies would not be so successful. Both the local and expatriate staff must respond flexibly to the individual situation of each enterprise, and give assistance when they can. The staff should also recognize when they cannot help and seek other avenues or agencies that can help in that situation.

Individual counselling or advice can play an important part in rebuilding a refugee's confidence and independence. It may be far quicker to tell a refugee what to do, than lead him or her to identify a problem and evolve a solution, but the latter is far more likely to be successful in the long term. This evolving approach encourages the refugee to actually follow the advice, and also he or she can then probably meet future problems without further external assistance.

W. WHAT ABOUT THE HOSTS?

W1. Introduction

Robert Chambers writes "Refugee relief organizations and refugee studies have refugees as their first concern and focus. Adverse impacts on hosts are relatively neglected... The poorer hosts can lose from competition for food, work, wages, services and common property resources [fuelwood, grazing land]". Although more educated hosts can benefit from increased employment and other benefits.

We suggest that there are positive and negative impacts on the host country, which are complex and individual to that country. If there are reasons to think that integration is likely, for instance a cultural similarity or tolerance between refugees and local people, then joint programmes are more possible. However, if thinking is towards return or resettlement, then dual-track or parallel programmes seem more appropriate. Certainly, any adverse impact on the poorer hosts should be alleviated and funders must be aware of this and perhaps fund local, refugee-affected area projects.

These are only some of the factors. It seems that as time progresses, the negative elements can build up, like competition in Pakistan. And so it is important to be aware of the actual impact of programmes on refugees, local people, and the local area, as well as the official positions about them. The arrival of refugees is bound to disrupt local people, and if assistance programmes- with the best of intentions - cause inequality by providing opportunities for refugees that are not available for the local people then the problems of a divided population can only get worse.

The processes for dealing with a refugee-affected area, rather than just with refugees, are still in their infancy. There are many examples of this work beginning, including the International Conference on Aid to Refugees in Africa (ICARA) initiatives, and many can start soon after the relief phase. But what types of initiatives are there?

W2. Separate or Integrated Programmes?

There seem to be many variations:

1. Refugee IG programmes taking in some local people - if refugees and locals are culturally similar this can work, as in the Quaker tie-dye business.

2. Local programmes involving refugees - ACORD in Port Sudan seems successful.

3. Refugee-affected area programmes, involving locals and refugees - The World Bank in Pakistan case study shows this. Others in Somalia and Sudan employ large numbers of the unskilled (poor?) in environmental or construction work.

4. Dual-Track Development - here agencies run similar parallel programmes, one for refugees, one for locals, like GTZ in Pakistan. This seems to be applicable if funding agencies for each can be found. In situations where the integration of refugees with locals is forbidden at any level, this represents the only way of trying to assist the concept of refugee-affected areas, without just looking at local area development.

There is not enough experience to be able to look more deeply at this issue yet, but it will need to be done soon.

X. ENDING THE PROJECT

X1. Introduction

Why write about ending the project? Often no mention is made of how the programme is to be ended in the objectives and yet how it is to end determines to some extent how it is to start. Is it going to be taken over by the government, is it going to fade away, leaving independent activities or will a local organization take over and carry on? So the agency's longer term goals as to what will happen to the programme once input from the agency has ended are important right from the start. A number of options present themselves for consideration:

X2. Government Takeover

Many agencies consider the strengthening of government institutions and the development of infrastructure, to be a priority objective. To this end local government employees may be trained, possibly with incentive payments from the agency; they may be seconded to the agency for a period of time; or the agency may employ and train its own local staff with a view to the government taking over their employment and the programme in the future. This objective is usually a result of the agency's concern at not setting up its own structures without heed to the host government's own efforts, and also in order to leave operating organizations behind, after expatriate withdrawal - so their efforts have long term benefits. The other advantages are that the agency, in working with the government (local and national) is less likely to become isolated in its work from the government's own development plans and, if successful, can indeed contribute to an improvement in the government's existing institutions.

There are potential drawbacks however. The agency is not working with a stable local population, but with people who are aliens and whose future, in their country of asylum, is uncertain. Also, the staff receiving "incentives" often leave when the payments are finally withdrawn. Given these variables, as well as the possible existence of ambivalent feelings between the refugees, the host population and the government, it may well be inappropriate to adopt the "institutionalization" of the programme, as a priority objective.

X3. Independent Local Takeover

For an agency interested in improving infrastructure as well as the immediate assistance to refugees, handover to an independent local group may prove to be a workable objective. This may be to a well established group or a group of local people and/or refugees which the agency has helped to set up. This has advantages in that a local group is likely to be much less bureaucratic than the government and therefore more easily able to respond to refugees needs. However, continued funding may well be more of a problem. If the programme takes the form of a revolving loan fund, including interest payments or charges towards the administrative costs, this may be reduced. But wholly self-financing revolving funds are few and far between, and we found none with refugees.

Interest payments can cause particular problems with governments in some places. They may see the payments as un-Islamic or exploitative of people who have already lost everything. Or the governments may see the interest rate is less than the local rate and so causing resentment in the local population. A balance has to be achieved.

If the agency has set up production workshops, particularly for those with special needs, such as the disabled, then self-sufficiency and independent local management may be even more difficult to achieve. The agency will need to commit itself financially, or find other sources of supportive finance, for the long term, after its own period of direct staff involvement.

Another consideration is the possible cultural pressures borne by members of the local management group from other members of their family or tribe. Field workers must be aware of the possibility of this happening, which might not be obvious when the project is being agency run. Particularly in the early stages of hand-over, the necessary support must be given to group members. During the preparation for hand-over, some agencies expel workers who discriminate; others carefully balance the ratio of staff to be the same as the camp or town.

Another possible obstacle to handing over management to a local group is that in many countries there is little or no tradition of independent voluntary groups and indeed they can be met with outright suspicion or discouragement. For example, Somalia has only three such voluntary or non-governmental groups as they are usually known, but there are many, traditional water-sharing or other groups, which could perhaps extend their activities, rather than change into the foreign concept of a voluntary organization.

X4. No Continuation after Agency Withdrawal

This strategy is very often viewed with disfavour by agencies who see no merit in setting something up with no prospects for a long term future. However, it is the refugees that matter and if their activities are continuing, then the programme is a success. The very fact that an agency remains may suggest failure - the programme should be terminated in a specific number of years, either because it has acheived its goals or because it has failed. Perhaps too many programmes continue beyond their useful lives?

This strategy of planning for a conclusion, with no continuation, may be one of the differences in doing development work with a possibly transient refugee population, as opposed to a relatively stable local population. The agencies and refugees think in shorter time-scales and indeed the whole situation may change if one of the durable solutions emerges.

Similarly, the agency may place emphasis on encouraging activities which can be transferred to whatever situation the refugees find themselves in the future, and try to avoid creating new infrastructure and so furthering the stability of camps. See the discussion on "Portability" in section C2. When the agency withdraws at the end of the programme timetable, the refugees then continue, independent of support, hopefully achieving a higher standard of living than previously, with good prospects for the future.

But this strategy does not have some of the advantages of other strategies - of improving the infrastructure in refugee camps and so creating a spill-over or educational effect on indigenous institutions. Moreover, there is little long-term job security for local staff, and the possible loss of a valuable trained team. Though often such people are in demand both by government and other agencies - the Primary Health Service in Somalia is largely staffed by people trained in the refugee camps.

Y. EVALUATION

Y1. Why Evaluate?

Evaluation of some sort is essential if anybody wants either to learn from the programme, or to change it, or to plan other programmes, at some time during its lifetime or when it has ended. With a new field, such as assisting refugees with income-generation, this learning process is very important. Evaluation does, however, take time and effort and nobody wants to spend time on a report that nobody reads!

It can also be extremely difficult to quantify the success or effectiveness of a programme. The best starting point for an evaluation, is to look at a programme's objectives and to see to what degree they have been achieved. So readers may refer back to section D. on objectives. The evaluation process will be easier if the objectives have been carefully thought through, avoiding abstract phrases. But, in any evaluation, it is also important to decide the answers to three questions:

1. <u>What to evaluate</u> Is it to evaluate the general goals, like strengthening local institutions or increasing certain groups' access to resources? Is it to evaluate the achievement of the objectives, such as numbers of successful businesses or improved technical or managerial skills? Or is it a restricted evaluation, using indicators for a part of the programme, like repayment levels, to see how the loan part of a programme is working?

Deciding to evaluate some aspect of the programme which has not been included in the original goals, objectives or indicators can be done, by setting these later, but must include a qualitative judgement of how things should have been done. This is rarely satisfactory.

2. <u>How to evaluate</u> Having decided what to evaluate, the following questions must be answered: How much time is allowed for the evaluation? What degree of precision is required? Once these questions have been answered, choices can be made between all the methods of evaluation. Is it by quantitative data, or qualitative data from project staff and participants or objective evaluation by outside consultants or a combination of these? Each has advantages and disadvantages and the choice must depend on local circumstances.

3. <u>Who is the evaluation going to and why?</u> Sometimes this is more important than what to evaluate, however, here we will treat it its normal place.

The most important audience, but the most neglected in carrying out evaluations, are the project field staff. They are in the best position to respond immediately to indicators, which suggest the need for change. This shows the connection between the reason for the evaluation and who it goes to. Here the reason is day-to-day management, so the evaluation goes to the field staff. The reason for a regular monthly or quarterly evaluation is for overall management and it should go to field directors, headquarters staff and where appropriate to co-ordinating or funding agencies. Annual and Project Evaluation Reports can have a variety of functions - decisions about the future or publicity or fund raising or to help others do similar work - and all have different audiences.

The aim is to produce an evaluation system, which can be used at every level, rather than produce special information for each audience, which may waste field staff time, in duplication, extra information collection, or administration.

Y2. A Possible Evaluation System for Refugee IG Projects

At present, our survey found no common system of evaluation indicators for refugee IG projects. The UNHCR in Pakistan showed the most consistency, using the numbers of direct and indirect beneficiaries and programme costs as their main indicators, with other indicators specific to each type of programme.

This data on numbers and costs is relatively simple to collect, and is effective in measuring the success of programmes which distribute rations or clothes or similar relief goods. But it is strange that there is not a general economic indicator for INCOME-generation. Why is this? The reason for having such a thing is to compare between agencies or for agencies to improve their own performance. The difficulty is what measure(s) can be used that apply to all these diverse types of IG? They must be simple, comparable between IG types and not over too long a time-scale.

Our aim here is not only to suggest a possible measure for the "Income" in IG programmes, but also to propose a system of evaluation, which although adding work initially, can be used by field workers and others for any level of evaluation required of them. Our proposal is a three level evaluation:

Primary Evaluation - simple statistics already applicable to most agencies.

Income and Self-sufficiency Evaluation - a new approach?

Particular Evaluation - specific to each project's objectives.

Y3. Primary Evaluation

Each programme year, the following ten statistics should be produced. The first seven are probably recorded anyway, but the last three are quite easy to record, if they are not already available:

(1) Number of direct beneficiaries
(2) Number of indirect beneficiaries (the exact categories should be stated, such as people receiving blankets, or the families of beneficiaries, or any extra jobs created)
(3) Total programme cost (including income)
(4) Cost of direct assistance given
(5) All local staff and related costs
(6) All expatriate staff and related costs
(7) Administration and other programme costs (all other costs, excluding items, 4, 5 and 6)
(8) Number of women direct beneficiaries
(9) Number of handicapped direct beneficiaries
(10) Numbers of any special sub-groups being direct beneficiaries (if this is relevant to the programme)

There may be difficulties, for example items such as transport could be in any category 4 to 7, but the aim is not meant to be rigid or create extra work, rather to begin an attempt at uniform measures. Simple statistics can then be prepared on each programme or between programmes, such as the cost per beneficiary, or the ratio of direct assistance to programme costs, the relationship between local and foreign staff costs, and so on.

The figures showing the assistance given for the last three categories to women, handicapped or members of special groups are very important. They are an attempt to make sure all programme staff think about these groups, in the same way that racial monitoring of employment practice is used to encourage employers at least to think about ethnic minorities and hopefully employ more. Not all programmes can include these groups, but they must be considered in the planning.

Y4 Income and Self-Sufficiency Evaluation

The above indicators are imperfect measures of the success of income-generating projects, since they contain no measure of the income generated. As stated before, there is no standard way of evaluating this income, yet the income or the self-sufficiency it tends to create, remain the goals of refugee IG programmes. So it is important to identify a measure which is related to these goals, without being so difficult to collect, or contentious in application, that it is of little practical value.

It may be useful to look to the accountant's measures of evaluating performance, in addition to the cost per beneficiary which has already been mentioned. These methods include calculating the following:

a) Total profits/Total expenditure. This is a very attractive approach in theory, but it can be very difficult to find out the actual profits of refugee enterprises.

b) Total Turnover or Sales. These can also be compared to the Total expenditure. Turnover is easier to estimate than the profits of a business, but if there are supply problems or a high turnover of unprofitable items, (and either can happen in refugee businesses), then such figures can be misleading.

c) Numbers employed. This is a reasonably easy figure to collect, but unfair to those projects helping businesses start, and if pursued by the project staff this could be detrimental to the long-term viability of the business created.

d) Value added. That is either the total of wages, salaries, withdrawals and profit or the Sales minus the purchased materials, supplies or services. This is a preferable measure to either profits or turnover, and includes an indication of the numbers employed. Nevertheless, it can be difficult to calculate and it needs to be evaluated some time (1 year?) after the assistance, advice or training. It is also not a good measure for relief substitution or other programmes which control most of their component parts, like wages and materials.

e) Rate of Return. This is comparing income received to the project costs, but is very similar to value added in calculation. Again some time-scale is needed.

It is not easy to produce a standard gauge of economic success suitable for all IG projects. But having looked at all these measures, the case studies and all the information from the respondents who sent in the data, we suggest two general indicators - the first being a simple cost per job, worked out from the figures in the primary evaluation. It must be admitted that this suits programmes that assist refugee enterprises better than those where the refugees are employed by the agency.

This same reason caused the rejection of value added and rate of return, as they are too specifically aimed at businesses and do not sufficiently account for programmes which are wholly or partly run by the agencies. So for the second measure of the income part of an income-generation programme we suggest an estimate of the ratio:

Main Income Received: The Total Cost of that Assistance.

By the "Main Income", we mean an estimate, as realistic as possible, of the increased income or wages of the "Direct Beneficiaries"; those recorded in the primary evaluation. To be fair to some programmes, this should also include other beneficiaries, in similiar positions as those directly benefitting, for example, from any extra jobs created, as shown in Example 1.

The timing of receiving the income compared to the cost of assistance is very important. Usually, this Main Income will be the total for the year AFTER the assistance has been received, especially for training projects, and for nearly all of the business programmes. However, for relief substitution and for projects where the agency pays the wages, the main income will be the wages earned during the year of assistance, by the refugees. In most cases, the time periods will be the programme years, rather than calendar or accounting period years, as it is the programme that is being evaluated. Shorter periods, such as the six months life of the Christian Outreach programme in Example 2. are also possible using this measure.

EXAMPLE 1. ACORD

ACORD helped 851 businesses, helping 1,250 people with jobs, each increasing their incomes by £S100 per month, from June 1984 to the end of 1985. Their success rate was 85% and programme costs were $750,000 per year. The average exchange rate over this period was £S2.45 per $.

Main Income = Income/participant x No. main participants x Success Rate

$$= \frac{£S100 \times 12 \text{ months}}{2.45 \text{ £S/\$}} \times 1{,}250 \times 85\% = \text{U.S.\$ } 520{,}408$$

Total Assistance Cost = Cost per year x No. of Years

$$= \$750{,}000 \times \frac{17 \text{ months}}{12 \text{ months}} = \text{U.S.\$ } 1{,}062{,}500$$

So the Ratio of Main Income: Total Assistance = $\frac{\$ 520{,}408}{\$ 1{,}062{,}500} = 0.49$

EXAMPLE 2. Christian Outreach

The Christian Outreach Weaving Programme lasted six months and cost a total of $12,500, with $2,000 paying for the expatriate part-time (authors' estimate), $1,000 on tools and equipment. Of the rest 11% was for the cotton, 89% for the wages of weavers, spinners, the watchman and the supervisor.

Ratio Main Income: Total Assistance = $\dfrac{\$9{,}500}{\$12{,}500} \times 89\% = 0.68$

EXAMPLE 3. AICF in Pakistan (with some information from ARC)

Assistance International Contre la Faim helped 795 businesses with tool kits, which created 1,129 jobs. The authors' estimate a minimum increase in their incomes of an average 1,000 rupees per month ($60). This assistance cost $170,400 (authors' estimate). According to the Austrian Relief Committee, with a similar programme, about half the refugees used the equipment fully, the other half used the equipment about half the time, giving a 75% success rate overall.

Ratio Main Income: Total Assistance = $\dfrac{1129 \times \$60 \times 12}{\$170{,}400} \times 75\% = 3.6$

This gives a "payback" period of about three months which is similar to a rate of return of 360%! The ARC case study is calculated in nearly the same way as this example, with slightly lower numbers of refugees and higher costs, giving a ratio of 1: 2.4.

Example 4. Chicken Project - Quakers in Somalia

The calculation on p.26 gave the best and worst case for the value of the Quaker assistance. The worst case was to treat the benefits as if all the chickens given had been sold. This gave a value of $4,620. The best case was that the refugees got a cash value for all their eggs, as if they were sold on the market. This gave a value of $9,200. Both calculations had already taken into account that one third of chickens were lost to predator animals or birds. The resulting average of about $7,000 was a fair estimate for the equivalent income the refugees received from the project, which cost $14,000. Remember that in this case the feed was free, because the chickens were free range, but in other projects the feed costs may have to be taken into account. Therefore:

Main Income: Total Assistance = $\dfrac{\$7{,}000}{\$14{,}000} = 0.5$

So how is this ratio calculated for all the eight types of IG projects?

In Relief Substitution and Development Investment projects, there are usually two benefits - the wages paid and the activity itself.

For relief substitution projects it is possible to calculate the value of the ratio for the wages of the direct beneficiaries, like Christian Outreach at 0.68 in Example 2. It is also possible to calculate, fairly easily, the value of the cloth produced for the refugees, who are the indirect beneficiaries. This cloth value is 4,167 m at 1 US $/m at a cost of $12,500, giving a ratio of 1:0.33. This shows clearly the double benefit of getting the refugees to produce their own goods; the money is used twice, and so the sum of the ratios should be more than one, if the project is more economically valuable, than just giving the money directly to the refugees.

In this case it is 0.68 + 0.33 = 1.01 and remember that the value of getting people involved and producing appropriate traditional cloth cannot be measured in economic terms.

A similar situation exists for Development Investment; two ratios for the wages and the value of the activity can be calculated, though the latter can be very difficult to estimate. The World Bank in Pakistan calculated a 12% rate of return on their investment, but it was an extremely complex calculation which involved working out the worth of the land before and after the environmental improvement.

The average wages were 62% of the costs, so after three years the sum of the ratios, which represent the value of the activity was: 0.62 + 0.12 + 0.12 + 0.12 = 0.98

For Income-Adding Starter projects, the numbers in the activity are likely to be too great for the income to be calculated by anything other than a small sample survey and an extrapolation of the results. Though gross calculations of the value of the activity may be possible, such as in the chicken project of Example 4. or other very rough calculations.

For Basic Skills Projects, both in agriculture and handicrafts, if the enterprise is agency-run, the wages and salaries paid are the "income". If it is an independent business, it can be treated like the other business assistance programmes. As always there are other measures possible, and these may be needed if the programme is partly agency-run and partly refugee-run.

For Business Starter and Business Assistance Projects, the main income might be calculated using the formula below, similar to that used in Examples 1. and 3. for ACORD, AICF and ARC:

Main Income = No. of jobs x Average increase in income x % Success

Where the incomes are more accurately known, as in programmes working in detail with one, or a small number of enterprises, then the formula below might be possible:

Income = Total Sales minus Total Costs

But these types of programmes seem rare with refugees, compared to local development initiatives. For any type of IG project, where the assistance is to new or existing businesses; the earnings of the owner and any employees, which is similar to the figure for value added, is the "benefit". For existing businesses, this benefit is the increase in the earnings, above what they were earning before the project.

Vocational Training and Employment Bureaux; the earnings of refugees who found employment, or started their own enterprises, using their skills, must be compared with the cost of training or running the bureaux. As with the other projects a measure of how much success each project achieved is necessary. It must be remembered that some of the refugees would have gained some earnings without the projects, but this may not be apparent, so it may perhaps be ignored as most refugees do not have many other options open to them.

So, we now have the means to measure economic success that we wanted in Y2., and it is fairly simple to calculate, although there are different ways of doing these calculations. The measure is comparable between different types of IG project. The final criteria is for the measure not to be over too long a time-scale - this separates the two fundamental extremes of IG projects:-

1. Those projects that only exist as long as the agency continues.

2. Those projects whose activities continue after the agency has finished giving that assistance.

The first extreme includes relief substitution, some development investment, some agriculture and handicraft programmes and occasionally other types of programmes. For these the sum of the wages and any other benefits should exceed the costs (i.e. sum of ratios >1.0), otherwise, it could be more cost-effective to give the money to the refugees. Unless, of course, there are strong social, not economic reasons for that IG programme.

The second extreme values those projects which aim at self-sufficiency. We suggest these should be valued each year over a three year period - as this is the usual time-scale that people can envisage with refugee populations. So, assuming that some refugees get more prosperous and some less, but overall if those refugees assisted acheive the same income levels in their second and third years as they did in the first, then the value of the ratio should be more than 0.33 in the year after assistance.

Hopefully these refugees will continue their businesses beyond the three years, but one should be cautious and not expect such continuation. Normally the value of the assistance would be calculated by a Discounted Cash Flow exercise in the second and third years, but this is complex and does not fit our aim of simplicity.

So how do our case studies do?

	Ratios
<u>Type 1.</u> (Should be greater than 1.0)	
Christian Outreach (Weaving and Spinning Wages)	0.68
(Value of the Cloth)	<u>0.33</u>
TOTAL	1.01
<u>Type 2.</u> (Should be greater than 0.33)	
Assistance International Contre la Faim (Toolits)	3.6
Austrian Relief Committee (Tool kits)	2.3
Quakers (Chickens - Income-adding Starter)	0.5
Quakers (Business Loans)	1.1
ACORD (Business Assistance Programme)	0.49

The Christian Outreach programme is our only example of programmes not designed to continue and gets just over the ratio value of 1.0. All the other programmes are designed for the refugees activities to continue without further assistance and are all over our suggested base line of 0.33.

The value of this ratio is that it looks at the assistance as an investment and compares this with the economic returns. A low ratio may be entirely justified, for instance, where work with a disadvantaged group is the objective or to give the products to other needy refugees, like the cloth just mentioned. Such objectives would be evaluated by other measures from the particular evaluation section.

However, if the ratio is high, it indicates some real success for an income-generating progamme. The best ratios may only be achieved with skilled refugees in countries with a relatively well-developed infrastructure, so it may be unfair to compare the ARC and AICF programmes in Pakistan with other programmes in Somalia and Sudan. It may be better to compare the ratios of programmes operating in the same country.

BUT these ratios are not "facts"; each ratio is an ESTIMATE, as realistic as possible, of the economic return of each project. Since each agency will calculate this in different ways, especially for different types of IG project, there is much room for discussion, argument and debate. This will lead, hopefully, to increased cost-effectiveness, which will benefit the refugees. Such discussions of these estimates need to be based on open figures and stated assumptions, if they are to be successful.

Clearly, the above calculations are greatly simplified, and the problems of data collection, particularly with refugees, make it nearly impossible to get anything other than an estimate. Nevertheless, it is better to make some attempt, than not even to try, since income-generation is primarily an economic activity and economic resources are being spent on promoting it: some form of cost/benefit analysis must be attempted, even of the simplest kind.

Y5. Particular Evaluation

There are certain evaluation measures, which are particular to one type of project and which are worth using, both to compare that project with other similar ones elsewhere, and to compare the performance of the same project over time. Most of these indicators may be self-evident, but for the sake of completeness we list the various types of project together with some of the indicators which it might be appropriate to use.

One word of warning: using indicators, which are costs, like numbers of items given or numbers of people trained, are *interim* indicators to be used initially, before a measure of the "return" is obtained. In IG projects, the real "return", on the investment of these costs, is the income or wages earned by the refugees. It is too easy to give away many useless items or train people for non-existent employment and then count the programme as a success!

1. Relief Substitution - The number of items produced, their production cost and perhaps a comparison cost to international prices or local prices.

2. Development Investment - The equivalent cost of the same works, if carried out by local or international contractors; some estimate of the environmental saving or of the long-term environmental benefits.

3. Income-Adding Starters - The numbers of items given, such as tool kits, chickens. The refugees should have passed some form of eligibility test to be able to use the items effectively. This is an interim measure, as it is very important not to use items given away as the only measure of achievement.

4. Basic Skill Utilization - The hectares farmed; the sales values of handicrafts; the "break-even points" or viability of enterprises.

5. Vocational Training and Production - Numbers of trainees starting and numbers successfully finishing the course, perhaps also the numbers at various stages or points in the course. Again these are provisional indicators, since training is a cost, both for trainees and trainers, the benefits only come when the skills are put to use.

6. Business Starter Schemes - the number and average value of assistance given; the numbers and types of requests; and how many use the equipment given. As before, the level of agency expenditure is no indicator of achievement.

7. Business Assistance Schemes - the success/failure rate; payback or repayment rate; general observation of economic activity, or specific observation of growth businesses..

8. Employment Bureaux - the numbers of applicants and those placed.

There are many other indicators. It may be appropriate for funding agencies to set standard criteria of achievement for the different types. Some measures, like success rates of the programme, are already contained within our suggestion of an estimated realistic ratio of Main Income to Cost.

Z. CONCLUDING COMMENTS

Z1. The Politics of Income-Generation

The refugees we are concerned with in this book have come from a poor country and they are in a poor country, almost certainly adding other problems for their hosts. In most cases, their exodus arose from a political situation, and that situation remains. They are not now in need of emergency relief, they are awaiting a solution and while they wait, it is hoped they may generate some income, but that is not ideal. The real solutions are political ones. It may be that in alleviating the immediate problems, those solutions are made less urgent. Perhaps agencies and individuals, as well as helping to solve these immediate issues, should also seek ways to help the refugees seek a long-term answer, as their assistance may delay solutions to the problem.

Z2. Speedy Income-Generation?

Many respondents felt that refugees could start some IG projects within months of arrival, if the conditions were right. If this is to happen, three conditions need to be satisfied:

1) Some record of the refugees' skills needs to be made at the initial registration. Ideally this should include the main skill or previous job with any subsidiary skills and the refugees' competence level in each. If this is done relief agencies can immediately identify the skills they need, whether builders or clerks, administrators or tailors. And later, these or other agencies can use the skills list to plan other IG projects.

2) Relief agencies must ask for some commitment from the refugees. This may mean asking the refugees to donate their labour to help to build health centres; to attend a training course as a condition of receiving free seeds; to do some cooking, if their child is receiving supplementary feeding. If food, clothes, medicines, education, utensils and housing materials, are all given out free, without asking for any commitment, it is far more difficult later to move towards genuine self-sustaining income generation.

3) Relief agencies should make time and perhaps establish a small budget for planning and training staff to start appropriate programmes as soon as the emergency phase ends.

None of this is easy and future IG possibilities might seem of minor importance during the emergency, when people have just been saved from total destitution. But a little thought and organization can bring many benefits later. It may even be that some emergency services and relief can be provided more quickly by using the refugees and local resources, than by relying on imported materials and labour and waiting for these to arrive.

Z3. The Balance of Income-generating Projects

Most IG projects are with men, in areas near towns, especially main towns, and often the projects have a lower proportion of minorities, such as handicapped or tribal sub-groups. All funding agencies and coordinating agencies, such as the UNHCR, the host government and others, should try actively to encourage agencies to be more balanced in their coverage of the refugee areas. Though each agency should review its own programmes and see if they are equitable towards women, rural refugees or one or more of these minorities.

Z4. Sharing Information

Our survey suggests that there is much to gain from more sharing of information between agencies. Such topics as "understanding the local and host cultures, ways of reaching particular groups, making IG more cost-effective" - all of these and many others would form useful seminars encouraging the exchange of experience between agencies in one country. Most of our case studies have acted as promoters of this sort of exchange and seem to have been successful.

This is not to say that the benefits of small, individual initiatives should be lost by efforts to coordinate or standardize - there are too many variables to be able to say one way is right and another wrong. Rather all agencies can learn from one another and since we found at least fifteen IG agencies in the countries with big refugee influxes, there may be much to share. Indeed this book is such an attempt to share, but cannot give the detailed background for each situation, that can only come from close personal contact.

Z5. A Final Comment

Finally, we should like to end by paraphrasing two replies to our questionnaires:

INCOME GENERATION IS ALWAYS DIFFICULT, YOU HAVE TO BE REALISTIC AND PREPARED TO MAKE MISTAKES -

BUT IT'S FUN AND IT CAN BE DONE.

METHODOLOGY

The research for this book was done between July and December 1986, with some extra information reaching us as late as May 1987.

Phase 1. Identification of possible agencies. During July to September known agencies were sent introductory letters explaining the research on refugee IG projects, asking for field addresses, for permission to contact the field staff and for any other contacts that the agencies had.

Phase 2. Package to field addresses. The package was sent between July and October and it contained an explanatory letter and three questionnaires. Both the letters and the questionnaires are reproduced in this Appendix, with the summary of all the respondents' replies.

Questionnaire A. was to examine the background and statistics of the agencies' IG programme, asking mostly for quantitative data.

Questionnaire B asked the field staff for their views on the more subjective, qualitative factors about the success of income-generating programmes.

Questionnaire C comprised twenty copies of a refugee business questionnaire for field staff to ask refugees.

In the accompanying letter, we also asked for any information that agencies could send us, if they did not have the time for one or more of the questionnaires.

Phase 3. Visit agencies in Europe to find information, discuss problems and identify the appropriate form for the final document. This process took place between August 1986 and May 1987.

Phase 4. Cross-check information. From October until May 1987, we tried to check our first thoughts and to substantiate for ourselves some of the information coming in to us. This included a field visit to one area. Pakistan was chosen, because the authors could follow up a UNHCR survey on income-generation there and they aleady had first hand experience of refugee IG projects in Somalia, Sudan and Kenya.

Phase 5. Sift information and draw up the final reports. The first drafts of the field studies were prepared in November, the book was edited between March and October 1987.

CONTACT LIST

The following organizations are all working to support refugee income-generation AND have responded to a questionnaire or visit. The visits in the UK and Pakistan account for the higher representation of these areas. Each organization responded either with a completed questionnaire or a full report of their activities. For this we would like to thank them all, as they form the basis of this book.

Special thanks are due to UNHCR in many countries, who are supporting much of this work, and particularly to UNHCR Geneva and Pakistan, who answered many questions in our field visits there.

ACORD (changing from EUROACTION ACORD)   or   ACORD Port Sudan
Francis House (3rd Floor)   P.O. Box 917
Francis St   Khartoum
London SW1P 1DQ; UK.   SUDAN

    See the Business Assistance Casestudy. ACORD also have a Somalia programme for 1972 drought refugees.

ACROSS (Association of Christian Resource Organisations serving Sudan)
Box 21033
Nairobi
Kenya

    ACROSS has a very wide ranging programme in the Sudan, including the following activities with percentages of the total cost:

Chadian Refugee Programme	16%	Construction Activities	14.8%
Agriculture and Rural Development	12%	Ugandan Refugee Program	12%
(this Ugandan scheme includes the business scheme whose form is on P.108)			
Emergency Relief	11.2%	Health Care	6.3%
Education and Literacy Work	4.8%	Water Development	3%
Community Engineering	2%		

ACTION AID
Hamlyn House,
Archway, London N19 5PS, U.K.

    The Action Aid programme in Somalia with refugees includes agriculture, education, tailoring, handicrafts and appropriate technology.

AFGHAN AID
c/o UNHCR, 1 Gul Mohar Lane
P.O.Box 767 University Town,
Peshawar, PAKISTAN

    The Afghan Aid programme includes health and personal counselling components as well as various relief subsitution projects making school bags, uniforms and tents, by able-bodied and handicapped women.

AFGHAN CULTURAL ASSISTANCE FOUNDATION
c/o UNHCR,
P.O.Box 1263
Islamabad, PAKISTAN

    ACAF give assistance to carpet weavers, including help with exporting.

ALL AFRICA CONFERENCE OF CHURCHES
Refugee Service
All Africa Council of Churches
P.O.Box 14205
Nairobi, KENYA

    The AACC help refugees in many ways, their IG projects include:
    Algeria - handicraft programme   Botswana - 10 businesses
    Djibouti - 68 vocational trainees   Kenya - 10 tailors
    Rwanda - A womens centre and a chicken project
    South Africa, Swaziland and Tanzania - farming and self-help projects
    Zambia - 6 businesses   Zimbabwe - 3 businesses

AMERICAN FRIENDS SERVICE COMMITTEE (AFSC)
1501 Cherry St, Philadelphia,
Pennsylvania 19102 , USA

    The AFSC have run IG programmes with refugees in Ethiopia, Mali, Palestine and Somalia, though none currently continue under AFSC. They prefer correspondence to USA, rather than to field staff, to save staff time.

ASSISTANCE INTERNATIONALE CONTRE LA FAIM (AICF)
Al-Ghalani Road
G.P.O.Box 319
Quetta, PAKISTAN

    See the AICF case study on giving tool kits in Baluchistan.

ASSISTANCE TO RESOURCE INSTITUTIONS FOR ENTERPRISE SUPPORT (ARIES)
c/o Harvard Institute for International Development (HIID)
1737 Cambridge St
Cambridge, Massachusetts 02138
USA

    USAID funded exploration and support to improve micro-enterprise development programmes - it includes some work with refugee programmes.

AUSTCARE
86-90 Bay St, Broadway
P.O.Box K359, Haymarket 2000
AUSTRALIA

    Helps to fund UNHCR and 14 member agencies of AUSTCARE - 7 of these agencies run 16 refugee IG projects in 14 countries. AUSTCARE tries in particular to address the long-term needs of refugees.

AUSTRIAN RELIEF COMMITTEE FOR AFGHAN REFUGEES (ARC)
80-D, Park Rd, University Town, Peshawar, Pakistan.
Mail Address: P.O.Box 489, GPO, Peshawar, PAKISTAN

    The ARC programme is detailed in the case study.

CATHOLIC RELIEF SERVICES
House 31B
Islamabad F7/1 Street 31,
PAKISTAN

>CRS have many programmes throughout the world, but we used details of this project, which helped train 96 women to produce childrens' clothing.

CHRISTIAN OUTREACH
34 St. Mary's Crescent
Leamington Spa
Warwickshire CV31 1JL
UK

>Besides the relief substitution weaving case study in Sudan, Christian Outreach have other training projects for refugees.

COMMISSION FOR AFGHAN REFUGEES (CAR = Pakistan Government Department)
c/o UNHCR, P.O.Box 30,
Quetta, PAKISTAN

>CAR in Baluchistan District are connected with the Pakistan Government's Small Industries Training Board. They run vocational training in 7 centres in 7 trades.

Church of South India Council for Technical and Vocational Training (CSI CTVT)
7 Avenue Rd
Mungambakkam
Madras 600 034, INDIA

>CSI CTVT gives technical training for Sri Lankan Tamils in 6 subjects.

Deutsche Gesellschaft fur Technische Zusammanarbeit (GTZ)
Domestic Energy Saving Project
P.O.Box 896, University Town
Peshawar, PAKISTAN

>GTZ give training, business help and loans for fuel saving stoves and ovens - see case study in section I. They also have a strong vocational training programme.

International Development Enterprises (IDE)
1901 Kipling, Suite 24
Lakewood, Colorado 80215
U.S.A.

>3 year donkey cart and rower pump business introduction programme in Somalia ended 1986. Other IDE projects exist, but no details available.

International Labour Organisation (ILO)
Small Enterprise Development Branch
CH-1211 Geneva 22
SWITZERLAND

>ILO have run and are running many IG programmes in developing countries. With refugees they are running several joint programmes with UNHCR (eg SPAREK - see later) and also four refugee IG programmes of their own:
>Costa Rica - Vocational training (900 trainees per year in 8 subjects).
>Pakistan - Construction programmes.
>Somalia - IG, self-reliance, chickens and soapmaking now handed over to newly created local voluntary agency.
>Sudan - Revolving loan fund.

INTERNATIONAL RESCUE COMMITTEE (IRC)
P.O.Box 504
University Town
Peshawar, PAKISTAN

>IRC have run many refugee programmes. In Pakistan, their IG projects include integrated self-reliance, handicrafts, poultry, vegetable gardening and a printing training workshop.

MENNONITE CENTRAL COMMITTEE (MCC)	MCC Somalia
21 South 12th Street	c/o UNHCR
Box M, Akron	P.O. BOX 2925
Pennsylvania 17501	Mogadishu
USA	SOMALIA

The MCC run at least six programmes with refugees; we included information from MCC Somalia on agriculture, training and small business loans. MCC Bangladesh helped some refugee enterprises and MCC Thailand ran resettlement job orientation. MCC El Salvador, Honduras and Mexico had no details available.

The OCKENDEN VENTURE
Guildford Rd
Surrey GU22 7UU
UK

>3 Programmes- In Pakistan a large relief substition project for quilts and school clothes, combines with an selling and export marketing centre. In Sudan, medical, job training, self-help and a handicraft centre for the disabled. And in Thailand, handicraft marketing and self-help.

OXFAM	and	OXFAM TRADING
274 Banbury Rd		Murdoch Rd, Bicester
Oxford OX2 7DZ		Oxon OX6 7RF
UK		UK

Oxfam have many refugee IG projects in Somalia, Zambia, Angola, Uganda, Rwanda, India and other countries.
Oxfam Trading gave useful information on refugee IG in HongKong.

PAKISTAN LIVESTOCK DEPARTMENT - Baluchistan
c/o UNHCR, P.O.Box 30,
Quetta, PAKISTAN

> The Department runs poultry, sheep and cow projects.

PARTNERSHIP FOR PRODUCTIVITY (PfP) - Somalia
P.O.Box 1012
Hargeisa, SOMALIA

> This PfP programme gave business assistance and technical training to refugees and Somalis, using local advisors and business people. However PfP International, which ran business advice programmes world wide was suspended in February 1987. Some of its projects are now being run by CARE, 660 First Avenue, New York NY 10016, U.S.A.

QUAKER PEACE AND SERVICE (QPS)
Friends House, Euston Rd,
London NW1 2BJ, UK

> QPS are running 3 refugee IG programmes - In Botswana, refugee rehabilitation, In Somalia, a camp based programme (see the case study) and in Western Sudan, a community development programme.

The SALVATION ARMY
Afghan Refugee Assistance Project
9/B- Rafiqui Lane
Peshawar, PAKISTAN

> Health work as well as vocational training, and marketing, especially leatherwork.

SAVE THE CHILDREN FEDERATION
54 Wilton Rd
P.O.Box 950
Westport, CT 06881, USA

> 4 Refugee IG Programmes - Crafts in Mexico, Small enterprises in Palestine, In Pakistan, small enterprises, credit, self-help, poultry, vegetable gardens, handicrafts and vocational training. Local enterprise and credit in Somalia. Other programmes mentioned, but no details.

SMALL INDUSTRIES DEVELOPMENT BOARD - Pakistan
c/o UNHCR, P.O Box 30,
Quetta, PAKISTAN

> Vocational training with about 500 boys making carpets, shoes and shawls.

SOS/PG - Belgium and Solidarite Afghanistan - Belgium
2 Rehman Baba Rd
University Town, Peshawar, PAKISTAN

> The SOS/PG main programme is Teacher Training but they also place apprentices in Pakistani and Afghani refugee workshops.

Special Programme for Assistance to Refugee Entrepreneurs in Kenya (SPAREK)
ILO Small Enterprise Development
P.O.Box 43801, Nairobi
KENYA

> A complex loan, advice and training programme covering micro-enterprises to fairly sophisticated businesses.

THREADLINES - Pakistan Textile Crafts Development Organisation
Supermarket F-6, P.O.Box 1348,
Islamabad, PAKISTAN

> Handicraft production and marketing (including export) from 6 centres by about 20,000 Pakistanis and 5,000 Afghan refugees.

United Nations Relief and Works Agency (UNWRA)
P.O.Box 19149
Jerusalem
via Israel

> 9 project businesses receiving loans and advice.

WOMENS EMBROIDERY PROJECT - Pakistan
c/o UNHCR, P.O.Box 30,
Quetta,
PAKISTAN

> High quality embroidery, run by one volunteer with up to 350 refugees. See ILO book "The Marketing Approach" by Susan Malick for case study.

WORLD BANK - Pakistan
c/o UNHCR, P.O.Box 767,
University Town, Peshawar,
PAKISTAN

> Large environmental improvement and employment scheme using mostly unskilled labour (70-90% refugees). See the case study in Section I.

WORLD ALLIANCE OF YMCAs - Young Mens Christian Associations.
Refugee and Rehabilitation Section
37 Quai Wilson
1201 Geneva,
SWITZERLAND

> A number of refugee programmes:
> Costa Rica - Home-school workshop (refugees from El Salvador).
> India - Tamil relief in Madapan.
> Kenya and Sudan - Vocational training for refugees.
> Thailand - Agriculture and weaving programme.
> Uganda - Support of displaced people in Uganda.
> West Bank - Vocational training in Jericho.

BIBLIOGRAPHY AND REFERENCES

As this is one of the first studies in this field, we have included some references for the sake of completeness, which may be difficult to obtain. This is not consistent with our wish to make this study easy to use. We hope the information will be useful for anyone carrying out further enquiries.

All Africa Conference of Churches Refugee Service, Handbook for Refugee Workers. AACC, Nairobi (1983)

All Africa Conference of Churches Refugee Service, One Refugee is One Too Many. AACC, Nairobi (1986)

Christensen H., Survival Strategies For and By Refugees - a six weeks study in Somalia. UNRISD, Geneva (1982)

Christensen H., Sustaining Afghan Refugees in Pakistan - Food and related social aspects. UNRISD, Geneva (1983)

CUSO/Thailand, Development of a Self-Help Assistance Programme for Displaced Cambodians - A Pilot Project -Report of Project Evaluation. CUSO, Canada (1982)

The Geneva Group, How to Run a Small Development Project, Intermediate Technology Publications, London (1986)

GTZ, Project Proposal for Vocational Training for Refugees and Sudanese Nationals. GTZ, Germany (1983).

Harrell-Bond B.E., Imposing Aid - Emergency Assistance to Refugees - A study in Sudan. OUP, Oxford (1986)

Harper M., Consultancy for Small Business - The Concept - Training the Consultants. I.T.Publications, London (1976)

Harper M., Entrepreneurship for the Poor - Programmes for Developing Countries. I.T.Publications, London (1984)

Harper M., Small Business in the Third World - Guidelines for Practical Assistance. John Wiley, Chichester (1984)

International Council of Voluntary Agencies, Timely Solutions - Voluntary Agencies and African Refugees. ICVA, Geneva (1984)

ILO/UNHCR, Tradition and Dynamism among Afgan Refugees - Income-generating activities for Afgan refugees in Pakistan. ILO, Geneva (1983)

ILO/UNHCR, Towards Self-Reliance - A Progamme of Action for Refugees in Eastern and Central Sudan. ILO, Geneva (1984)

ILO, The Marketing Approach - Planning income and employment generation for rural women. Susan Malick. ILO, Geneva (1984)

International Migration Review (Vol.20 No:2) Special Issue Refugees: Issues and Directions. Center for Migration Studies, New York (1986)

Kibreab G., Reflections on the African Refugee Problem - A Critical Analysis of Some Basic Assumptions. Scandinavian Institute for African Studies - Research Report No.67, Uppsala (1983)

OXFAM The Field Directors Handbook - A Oxfam Manual for Development Workers. OUP, Oxford (1985)

OXFAM, A Manual of Savings and Credit for the Poor of Developing Countries. Oxfam, Oxford (1987)

PLAN (Foster Parents Plan International Inc.) Income-Generating Projects of Small-Scale Development Organisations: A Field Study.

SIDA, Developing Entrepreneurs - An evaluation of Small Scale Industry development in Botswana 1974-84. SIDA, Stockholm. (1986)

Szal R.J., considerations in the Design of Employment -Generating Activities, Migration News No.1 (1984)

Thorogood B., Income-generating Projects, "Disasters" Vol.5 No 3. (1981)

UNHCR, Refugee Resettlement - A survey of Training Priorities in Thailand. CCSDPT, Bangkok (1986)

UNHCR, Handbook for Social Services - see Annex 9 on a checklist for self-employment projects, (1984)

UNHCR, Review of Income-Generating Projects for Afghan Refugees in Pakistan, Yvette Stevens, Technical Support Section UNHCR Geneva (1986)

UNWRA: Past, Present and Future. UNWRA, Vienna (1986)

VOICE (Voluntary Organizations in Community Enterprise), Income-generating Projects - A Training Manual, Zimbabwe

YMCA World Alliance/UNHCR, Guidebook for Action (Refugees and Rehabilitation). YMCA World Alliance, Geneva (1985)

COVERING LETTER TO AGENCIES SENT WITH THE QUESTIONNAIRES

This letter was sent from Cranfield School of Management and replies came in between July 1986 and May 1987

We understand that you are involved in assisting refugee enterprise. We are trying to produce a manual on the range of possibilities in this area. Despite the size of this package, we are very interested in hearing from you - your time allowing.

Between 1982 and 1985 we were involved in one large refugee camp with a loan/advice scheme, and later in training local business advisors to help refugees, both in Somalia. So we do know about pressures and workloads and we offer an "if you have not the time" alternative for the three parts of the enquiry.

Now we are on a short-term contract, working with Malcolm Harper of the Cranfield School of Management. The enquiry covers programmes for refugee business/enterprise/income generation. We are well aware of the many variables and constraints of these programmes and the lack of guidance for field workers, based on the positive and negative experiences of others. We hope the manual will provide a useful reference for refugee enterprise assistance programmes in the future.

We apologise for this arriving 'out of the blue' and it would be of enormous assistance if you could complete all aspects. But any help, however small, would be appreciated.

* * * * * * * *

AGENCY PROGRAMME QUESTIONNAIRE

QUESTIONNAIRE A : Background and Statistics. This will give us a comparison between all the programmes which include some business/enterprise/ income generating for refugees.

If you have not the time - Please send us a range of your reports giving objectives, practice and results. We will refund postage, if necessary.

QUESTIONNAIRE B: Factors Affecting Success. This is the main part of our survey (although it needs the background). Please answer this as thoughtfully as you can - use extra paper if you need to.

If you have not the time - Please send a short note outlining what you fel are the important factors in the success and failure of such a refugee programme.

Do send Sections A and B back before the refugee business questionnaire, if possible.

REFUGEE BUSINESS QUESTIONNAIRE C :

We cannot visit all programmes, but we would like to get a feel for the different circumstances that refugees are in. Enclosed are 4 bundles of 5 questionnaires; if it is appropriate, we can offer recompense to your staff, up to a total of $50 per programme. If possible, could each bundle be a separate group - eg,

1. Not in your programme
2. More successful businesses
3. Less successful businesses
4. Women
   etc, etc

The groupings are up to you, but please let us know on return of the completed forms. Going through the notes with the interviewers would also be helpful.

<u>If you have not the time</u> - Pleas send a short note of the difficulties facing refugees in business.

If you wish:

a. Details of this enquiry after completion
b. To be involved further, or
c. Any advice or assistance that we may be able to give (no promises)

please say so in your reply.

Thank you.

Yours sincerely

CHRIS AND CLARE ROLFE

<u>Note</u>: The terms business, enterprise and income generating are used interchangeably to include all such activities. Please use extra paper, if necessary.

AGENCY PROGRAMME QUESTIONNAIRE - A Summary of Replies

All programmes include some refugee income-generation parts, with refugees from poor countries and now in poor countries.

QUESTIONNAIRE A : BACKGROUND AND STATISTICS

Basic Information

1. Organisation name: *Introductory letters were sent to 107 Organisations. 79 Organisations were followed up by a questionnaire or visit.*
2. Field address: *These 79 Organisations run at least 153 programmes in 41 countries.*

									TOTALS
AFRICA :	Algeria	1	Botswana	3	Chad	1	Djibouti	1	
	Ethiopia	3	Kenya	8	Rwanda	1	Somalia	9	
	Southern Africa	7	Sudan	20	Tanzania	4	Uganda	2	
	West Africa	10	Zaire	2	Zambia	4	Zimbabwe	2	78
AMERICAS :	Belize	1	Chile	2	Costa Rica	3	El Salvador	2	
	Honduras	2	Mexico	2	(However, no Americas programme returned a completed questionnaire with good details)				12
ASIA :	Bangladesh	1	Hong Kong	1	India	5	Pakistan	22	
	Thailand	21	Vietnam	2	(However, Thailand does not permit self-reliance programmes to deter incoming refugees, but does allow training and self-help)				52
MIDDLE EAST:	(Only one programme returned completed questionnaires)								11
									153

3. Respondent name: *Not Applicable.*
4. Respondent position: *Most were returned by Field Directors or Head offices.*
5. Outline all the activities of your programme (concentrating on the enterprise components)

Of the 153 programmes:
- *31 sent in full details (See Contact List)*
- *118 sent in some details*
- *4 sent in no details, other than an address.*

Of the 149 programmes with
- *30% were Income-Generation Only*
- *70% had other non-I.G. parts (In decreasing order - Health, then Food, then Education)*

I.G. TYPE	NO.	Sub-type
1. RELIEF SUBSTITUTION	8	
2. DEVELOPMENT INVESTMENT	4	- Infrastructure
	4	- Environment
3. INCOME ADDING STARTERS	25	
4. BASIC SKILL UTILISATION	13	- Handicrafts
	13	- Agriculture
5. VOCATIONAL TRAINING AND PRODUCTION SCHEMES	39	
6. BUSINESS STARTERS	33	
7. BUSINESS ASSISTANCE	9	
8. EMPLOYMENT BUREAU	1	
TOTAL	149	

Background

Background Table (please answer relevant columns - appropriate estimates acceptable)

(Numbers of Organizations Answering Questions)

			AVERAGE No. (RANGE)		BUSINESS PROMOTION	
			TOTAL	TOTAL REFUGEE	NON-REFUGEE	REFUGEE
(23)	6.	Programme annual budget (U.S. $)	963,000 (11,000 – 9 million)	830,000 (11,000 – 8 million)	43,500 (0-1 million)	720,000 (6,750 – 8 million)
(21)	7.	Lifespan of programme (start date - end date) (in months)	42	38	4*	37
(17)	8.	Expatriate staffing (in full-time equivalents)	2.5	2.5	0*	2.1
(21)	9.	Local staffing (in full-time equivalents)	81* (2-1,000)	75* (2-900)	5*	70 (1-900)
(20)	10.	No. of sites you work in (eg, towns, camps, etc)	18* (1-80)	18* (1-80)	1*	18*

*(In Questions 6-10, * = Care Needed in Interpretation)*

11. Outline the funding sources for your programme (eg, 50% UK Government, 30% voluntary, 20% UN): *(Contributions to Funding greater than 30%)*

    (27) UNHCR 18, Voluntary 16, Own Govt 4, Host Govt 2, Other Govt 4, ILO 2.

12. Outline the roles of your staff:

    (20) As Trainers 14, As Field Staff 14, As Managers 6, As Support Staff 1
    (Although presumably all agencies have administrative or personal support staff)

13. How are your staff trained?

    (15) On-the-Job 11, Internal Courses 6, Already Trained 4, Sent Abroad 1.

14. How large is the target area(s) for your programme?

    (17) All of Country 1, All of Region 1, Most of Region 7, Some of Region 4, One Town/Camp 4.

Refugee Background

			AVERAGE (RANGE)
(12)	15.	How many refugees are there in your target area(s)?	750,000 (41,000 – 2.5 million)
(12)	16.	How many refugees in your target area(s) are in camp(s)?	613,000 (41,000 – 2 million)
(12)	17.	How many refugees in your target area(s) get food aid?	533,000 (17,000 – 1.75 million)

Refugee Business Programme

(Numbers of Organizations Answering Questions)

(Note: 4 large handicraft projects distorted the figures – so the first column excludes these)

AVERAGE (in last 12 months)

		12 Projects	ALL 16 Projects
(16)	18. How many refugee businesses have you helped directly?	318	852
(16)	19. In these businesses how many refugees have you helped directly?	443	945

Since you started, how many of those refugee businesses were:

		12 Projects	ALL 16 Projects
(16)	20. Existing businesses?	13%	4%
	New businesses using refugees' previous skills?	50%	85%
	New businesses requiring refugees to have new skills? (Usually after completing Training)	37%	11%
(16)	21. Production-type businesses?	40%	81%
	Service-type businesses?	37%	12%
	Retail-type businesses?	23%	7%
(16)	22. Solely with women?	18%	67%
	Include women? *In addition to those businesses only with women.*	3%	1%

(16) 23. Include handicapped? *Average 3 Handicapped people per programme.*

(16) 24. Since you started, how many refugee business requests for assistance have you had?
An average of 16% more requests, than assistance given; but large range from 0% - 500%

(47) 25. Please include a list of the types of businesses assisted
See Section P. for a list of all these businesses.

Financial Assistance

26. If you give grants:

		Country of Programme					
		INDIA	PAKISTAN 1	PAKISTAN 2	PAKISTAN 3	PAKISTAN 4	PALESTINE
(6)	a. What is the total number of grants per year?	100	81	795	409	1,000	9
(6)	b. What is the average amount each? (U.S. $)	14	65	121	130	322	2,000

(Numbers of Organisations Answering Questions)

Country of Programme

27. If you make loans:

	RURAL				URBAN		
	Pak.	Pak.	Som.	Sudan	Kenya	Sudan	Zambia
a. What is the total number of loans per year?	50	76	22	85	25	700	9
b. What is the average amount each? (U.S. $)	125	135	120	178	5,790	250	3,000

(7) a. What is the total number of loans per year?

(7) b. What is the average amount each? (U.S. $)

(7) c. Are the repayments monthly, seasonal or other? Usually monthly

(4) d. What is the average repayment period (eg, 12 mths)? 16 months

(4) e. What is the approximate % of loans in arrears? 18% average

(4) f. What is the approximate % of loans unlikely to be repaid? 10% average

(4) g. Do you charge interest - what percentage? 0%; 0%; 5%; 13%

(8) h. What contract/security do you require? See Section U.6.

(5) 28. Briefly describe your lending system (eg, use of banks, revolving fund, savings clubs, etc)
Revolving Fund 3; Local Loan Committee 1; Funds return to other projects 1.

Non-Financial Assistance

(17) 29. Which of the following methods of non-financial assistance do you use in assisting refugees? Please give the number of businesses assisted per year, adding comments if you wish. See Section V. for details.

(10) 30. What are the primary and other objectives, goals or aims of your refugee business/income generating programme? See Section Y. for details.

(9) 31. What criteria do you use to choose whom you help?
Using —   Surveys 1; Working Experience 2; A Loan Committee 1.
Observing —   Viable Businesses 2; Productive Businesses 1.
For Special Cases — Low Income 3; Unemployed 2; Widows 1; Orphans 1; Special Hardship 1.
Other Conditions — Family Responsibilities 2; Residential 1.

(7) 32. What evaluation criteria/indicators do you use for your objectives/goals/methods? Please give the criteria and any results, even if preliminary. Business Success/Failure Rate 4; Loan Repayment Rate 2;
One Comment each for :- Numbers of Requests; Increased Income; Using Equipment Given; General Observation of Economic Activity.

(7) 33. Do you know any other agencies doing refugee business/enterprise/income generation in your area? Please give a contact name and address. On average three other agencies were given.

QUESTIONNAIRE B : FACTORS AFFECTING SUCCESS

* Please give a value (0-5) for the relative importance of the following factors in the <u>success</u> of planning or running a business/enterprise programme for refugees

  Very important=5 : Important=4 : To be included=3 : To be considered=2 : An unimportant factor=1 : Of no value=0. Please answer all

RETURNED

FROM: Pakistan 10; Sudan 5; Somalia 2; Kenya 1; Palestine 1; Africa Desk 1 = TOTAL 20

BY: Field Directors 13; Regional Desk Officers 4; Ex-Field Directors 2; Researcher 1 = 20

The average for each question was calculated and put in the following ranges:

* RANGE *	AVERAGES	QUESTIONS
LOW	2.5 → 2.8	2, 16, 17, 22
LOW TO AVERAGE	2.9 → 3.2	4, 10, 11, 21
AVERAGE	3.3 → 3.5	5, 6, 7, 8, 12, 13, 15, 18, 19
AVERAGE TO HIGH	3.6 → 3.7	1, 14, 19
HIGH	3.8 → 4.2	3, 9, 20

RELATIVE IMPORTANCE VALUE

Initial Factors

1. THE LOCAL AVAILABILITY OF NATURAL RESOURCES → AVERAGE TO HIGH (3.75)

   How important is this factor to planning and running a programme for refugees?
   Your view:

   Very important for rural refugees and those refugees with traditional skills;
   Not so important for ex-urban or self-settled refugees or in countries with wide access to goods.

2. THE EDUCATIONAL LEVEL OF THE REFUGEES → LOW (2.8)

   How important is this?
   Your view:

   Not too important - specific training covers most business needs, though basic reading, writing and maths can help. Some evidence well qualified refugees not good at I.G.

3. THE SKILL LEVELS OF THE REFUGEES → HIGH (3.8)

   How important are these?
   Your view:

   Very important to know the skill levels of the refugees - to plan projects and to plan training. All people have skills - it is the basis of project success.

4. THEIR URBAN OR RURAL ORIGIN → LOW TO AVERAGE (3.2)

   What difference does this factor make?
   Your view:

   Only important in the initial planning. If the refugees have an Urban origin —
   More experience, easier adjustment to cash economy and opportunities - many go straight to towns.
   If Rural origin — more help needed, perhaps continuing community support from their elders.

RELATIVE
IMPORTANCE
VALUE

5. WHETHER THE REFUGEES ARE SELF-SETTLED OR IN A CAMP → AVERAGE (3.4)

   Do the similarities of being refugees outweigh the differences?
   Your view:

   Camp refugees have the constraints of bureaucracy, logistics and aid style, which may lead to dependency, though they may have better food, health, etc. Self-settled refugees = different "breed" - more motivation.

6. HOW LONG THE REFUGEES HAVE BEEN IN THE HOST COUNTRY → AVERAGE (3.5)

   Is there a best time to start business/income generating projects?
   Your view

   Very good to start early, but not before an "adjustment period" of 6 months - 1 year. Five replies mentioned start at 2 years. Four years after arrival "dependency" can start, but this depends on aid style.

7. THE CLOSENESS OF THE LINKS WITH THE LOCAL COMMUNITY → AVERAGE (3.5)

   Some refugees have family links, others are in an alien environment. Is it important?
   Your view:

   With small numbers of refugees, family links can provide good support. With larger numbers, it is initially easier for those refugees with links, but resentment from local people increases, unless they are also assisted. If no links - refugees have to succeed in business.

Operational Factors

8. THE SIZE OF THE MARKETS ACCESSIBLE TO THE REFUGEES → AVERAGE (3.5)

   Some are entirely camp dependent, others locally dependent, but is the size important?
   Your view:

   Obviously the bigger the markets accessible, the better for I.G. projects. Perhaps initially camp-based I.G. should start with Relief Substitution or small grants until the local or Host Government situation is known. Eventually some economic integration better for all.

9. THE OPPORTUNITIES ALLOWED BY GOVERNMENT FOR REFUGEES → HIGH (3.9)

   Like Q7 and Q8, there is a big variation in opportunities for refugees - is it important?
   Your view:

   All countries have some zenophobia and therefore some restrictions; Third World countries seem less restrictive than most. Agencies should try to increase the options for individuals and families sensitively, until told to stop, by working with Governments carefully. Though some respondents said to beware of "big" options.

RELATIVE
IMPORTANCE
VALUE

10. THE SIZE OF THE OPERATIONAL BASE OF THE PROGRAMME ⟶ LOW (3.2)

Is it important that the programme is organised on a regional/national basis or on a local (one camp/one town) basis?
Your view:

A specific local base, or area, is much preferred (10 replies). With large numbers of refugees, many independent local bases, well coordinated, are favoured, though difficult. But are N.G.D.'s good at large I.G.?

11. THE TYPE OF OPERATIONAL BASE OF THE PROGRAMME ⟶ LOW (3.1)

Is it important that the programme is specifically for business, or is part of a wider programme?
Your view:

It seems to be difficult to mix relief work and self-sufficiency programmes. If the I.G. assistance is relatively simple (small loans/tool kits), then the cultural knowledge built up by, say a Health Programme, can produce a successful project addition. If the IG is complex (Business Analysis), then experienced IG agency or personnel are needed. However, "Flexibility is the key".

12. THE SIZE OF THE ENTERPRISE/ACTIVITIES ⟶ AVERAGE (3.4)

Should the emphasis be on group or individual enterprises - why?
Your view:

Individual enterprises seem more successful - for cultural reasons, speed in starting and less disputes. Some enterprises only in groups - mass quilt-making, workshops, etc. Women seem better in groups than men.

13. THE TYPE OF TARGET GROUP ⟶ AVERAGE (3.5)

Should you assist potential entrepreneurs (who already have some skills/capital) or target the poorest or other groups (handicapped, women, etc)?
Your view:

Always a Dilemma. Four said target the poorest and accept the constraints of skill, education, etc. Eight said target both, aim for poor (eg by maximum loan), but useful to have entrepreneurs example and viability.

14. THE CONTINUATION OF THE PROGRAMME AFTER AGENCY WITHDRAWAL → AVERAGE TO HIGH (3.6)

Is it important to plan for a continuing service or to leave independent activities?
Your view:

Initial programmes should plan for independent activities, useful to the refugees now and in future. As the situation stabilises, emphasis should change to creating an independent, locally run service, which itself creates independent activities. The agencies long-term goals important, in choosing which path. Whichever is taken, it must be flexible to market and situation changes.

RELATIVE
IMPORTANCE
VALUE

15. THE TYPE OF TRAINING PROVIDED → AVERAGE (3.3)

Should the programme concentrate on production training,
management/financial training or a mix?
Your view:

Too many I.G. programmes run only production courses, though in most cases management training needed also. If the refugees are low skilled, training in both is difficult. The right mix is important.

16. NEW OR "OLD" BUSINESS EMPHASIS → LOW (2.5)

Is it important that support usually concentrates on
previously learned skills in existing businesses, or should
encouragement be given to new types of enterprise?
Your view

The viability of the business is more important than whether it is "New" or "Old".
Start with previously learned skills, for speed and viability, then build on these skills.
Training for new skills is more difficult, but can help some groups with new opportunities.

17. AN EMPHASIS ON 'PORTABLE' BUSINESSES → LOW (2.8)

To plan for refugees' return or transfer (and for acceptability to host governments as non-permanent residents) - how
important is 'portability'?
Your view:

Answers vary from "irrelevant" to "very". It should be thought about during the planning process, especially if there is a possibility of return - even if only in refugees minds.

18. IS 'DEPENDANCY' A FACTOR? → AVERAGE (3.5)

Refugees are often labelled as 'dependant' either as a
natural reaction to loss or as a result of the relief process.
How important is planning for this factor?
Your view:

Both causes of dependancy mentioned above are seen as real. Hence all programmes, not just I.G., need to look for ways to increase dignity, self-reliance and independence.
If dependancy shows in alienation or depression, then it is too late for enterprise.

19. REFUGEE INITIATION → AVERAGE TO HIGH (3.6)

How important is it that businesses are started on refugees'
own initiative?
Your view:

Initiatives by refugees should be supported and they work better than outside initiatives.
However most programmes are outside initiatives as refugees may have limited flexibility, unfocussed enthusiasm or be affected by the new situation or dependancy factors.

RELATIVE IMPORTANCE VALUE

20. REFUGEE PARTICIPATION → HIGHEST (4.1)

How important is refugee participation in the planning, staffing and management of the enterprise programme?
Your view:

Participation is the most important factor, but it is interpreted differently — Participation means "all staff are refugees" to "having refugee representatives" to "training needed at all levels."

21. IS LOCAL DISADVANTAGE A FACTOR? → LOW TO AVERAGE (3.2)

If refugees are given grants, loans or training which are not available to local people - is this a problem? Could integrating programmes help?
Your view:

Often refugees have better resources than local people in Less Developed Countries, but solutions depend on political/cultural factors. Conditions on Relief Aid may stop Parallel Funding for refugee-affected areas, but such joint or integrated programmes are better and are increasing.

22. MOST REFUGEES HAVE LOW CAPITAL AND SECURITY → LOW (2.5)

Is this a factor decreasing the success of enterprises, or can it be planned for?
Your view:

This factor HAS to be planned for and CAN be planned for.

(NUMBER OF REPLIES)

FOR THE NEXT THREE QUESTIONS, PLEASE RANK THE FACTORS YOU IDENTIFY

23. Please list any other factors that you think are important to the success of a refugee business/enterprise programme

1.) Knowing the economic/cultural/traditional background of the refugees (7)
2.) Time Factor - longer time scale for consistency, follow-up, picking right time to start (Speed = Failure) (6)
3.) Use "Developmental" Style - more participatory, charge for services, don't give grants, use revolving loan funds. (4)

24. Please list any other factors that you think can lead to the failure of a refugee business/enterprise programme

1.) Failing to understand the economic/cultural/political background of the host country (4)
2.) Camp/Refugee Administrative structure not set up for I.G. (e.g. too authoritative). (4)
3.) Inadequate supplies, capital and equipment at the beginning or as a continuing problem (4)

25. Please list the factors that refugees themselves think are important to the success of their businesses (rank them according to your perception)

1.) Access to reliable sources of money. (4)
2.) Access to travel, supplies, property and premises. (2)

26. Are there any other lessons learned or comments you would like to mention?

Success is due to the skills of staff - flexibility, openness, reliability and respect (3 replies)

Success is due to choosing good field staff and participants (3 replies)

SINGLE REPLIES

- Use the Simplest Approach Possible.
- Even the most desparate people retain their capacity to care for themselves and their families - this must be enhanced.
- Success comes from the willingness, experience potentialities and the physical abilities of the refugees.
- One Factor = The People. We must use "community adrenaline" to take on change and to take up ideas.
- One Factor = Reactionary Refugees. The refugees are both open to change and they return to traditional customs - the agencies must watch for this.
- There is greed and dishonesty.
- Sometimes there is a desire in agencies to do something... anything.
- Agencies cannot risk leaving some tasks to refugees, even if that task is theoretically good for development.
- Alienation is important - a camp is an artificial environment.
- Camps = "Total" Institutions, like prisons and hospitals, where the needs are defined by someone else and this leads to dependancy.
- (The Host Country) gains and loses by taking the refugees; it is economically gaining at the moment, but may lose in the long run.
- Most businesses fail - but it is a learning process for innocent refugees to meet innocent aid workers.
- You cannot escape supply and demand, relationship and competition.
- Perhaps we should include an element of savings into I.G. projects?
- Give grants and assist them (the refugees) to death!
- Refugees always come to us, thinking if they get a BIG loan to start, then they will be rich - it's a difficult myth to dispel.
- These mad, white people coming to help them are very, very rich (even if they are not).
- It's Quite Fun. It Can Be Done. But you have to be realistic and prepared to make mistakes.

Thank you

QUESTIONNAIRE C. – REFUGEE BUSINESS

Questions for Interviewer

1. Organisation

No.	Country	Symbol	No. of Refugees	Situation
1	KENYA	K	19	Self-Settled in capital Nairobi.
3	PAKISTAN	P	35	Camps and Towns.
1	PALESTINE	Pl	6	Refugees in camps and towns.
2	SOMALIA	So	31	In camps only.
2	SUDAN	Su	33	Self-Settled in Town + 13 in settlements.
TOTAL 9	–	–	124	–

2. Interviewer name <u>Average 2 each organisation.</u>

3. Area or place <u>Average 3 each organisation.</u>

4. Is refugee business assisted – with what?

(In Section 4.2. this information is reworked slightly differently from the categories here.)

Equipment or Loan Only	60
Training or Advice Only	2
Both Equipment/Loan and Training/Advice	38
Neither = No Assistance (14 from Somalia)	24
TOTAL	124

Questions for Refugees

5. Man or woman <u>91 men and 33 women</u> (leader, if a group business)

AVERAGES	K	P	Pl	So	Su	Women	ALL
6. Your age in years	39	33	33	36	3	33	36
7. How many years have you been a refugee?	9	4	27	6	8	7+	7+

Background (+ Means Palestinians excluded from average)

	K	P	Pl	So	Su	Women	ALL
8. How many years have you received food rations?	0	1	26	6	1	3+	2+
9. How many adults depend on your money (excluding you)?	1	3	0	3	3	2+	3+
10. How many children depend on your money? (Grants given only to NEEDY Palestinian Families)	3	4	5	4	5	3+	4+

11. How did you earn money before? 104 had some experience before – Women do sewing/cooking as job now. 15 had no experience and 5 were students before.

Business

12. How do you earn money now? Give main way, other ways and details, including where :-

Tailor/Cloth Sellers	26	Water Sellers	5	Quilt/sweater makers	3
Shopkeepers	17	Shoemaker/menders	5	Chicken farmers	3
Teashop/Restauranteurs	11	Farmers	4	Butchers	3
Bakers	9	Potters	3	Builders	2
Blacksmiths	9	Car Repairers	3	Hairdressers	2
Carpenters	8	Radio/Watch menders	3	Other Individual Businesses	8

8 of these refugees have two unrelated jobs – the main one was used in this list.

Starting Up

13. When you started this business, where did you learn the skills?

    From parents/family   = 39%   From own business before = 33%
    From training here   = 24% m From training elsewhere   = 36% m
    From working here   = 21% m From working elsewhere   = 29% m
    Any other answer*   = 2%
    * please put details in Question 26

14. When you started this business, where did you get your machines, tools, or animals?

    Brought with you   = 19%   Borrowed or hired (not with loan) = 10%
    Bought by or for you = 66%   Do not use tools,
    Any other answer*   = 0%   machines or animals
    * please put details in Question 26

    — 5% very small tools ie needles
    — 4% hand craft only
    — 3% simple shops - no scales.

15. When you started this business, where did you get your money from?

    From home   = 24%   Borrowed from family   = 11%
    Gift from family   = 7% w   Borrowed from refugees = 7% m
    Gift from refugees   = 2%   Borrowed from locals   = 6%
    Gift from locals   = 2%   Borrowed from agency   = 36%
    Gift/grant from   Saved while refugee   = 35%
    agency (Grant not usually cash) = 9%   Any other answer*   = 1% — Did not need money to start
    * please put details in Question 26

	K	P	Pl	So	Su	Women	ALL
16. How much money did you need to start? U.S. $	4,363	167	2,517	166	261	286	949

Running Your Business

	K	P	Pl	So	Su	Women	ALL
17. How much money comes to your business each month? U.S. $	746	103	503	242	297	164	307
18. How much money do you keep or use for you and your family each month? U.S. $	162	45	137	47	111	54	86
19. How many family members work for you?	0.3	1	0	1	1	0.7	0.9
20. How many people work for you outside your family?	2.4	1	0	0.1	1	0.5	1

21. Whom do you sell to?

    Refugees = 80%   Local people = 77%
    Agency   = 19%   Other   = 2% Businesses stopped temporarily

    (91% of women sell to refugees; 20% of refugee businesses sell only to refugees; 56% of refugee businesses sell to both refugees and local people only; 13% sell only to local people)

    KEY — m = mostly men ; w = mostly women.

Problems

22. When you started what were your biggest problems?

Getting money for business	= 75%	Not enough sales	=	32%
Getting supplies	= 35%	Too many businesses the same as yours	=	15%
Finding a good place(s) to sell	= 21%	Workers	=	3%
		Your lack of skills	=	12%
Transport	= 7%	Records	=	3%
Fuel	= 0%	Laws/regulations	=	5% m
Tools/machines	= 20%	Other	=	1% – seasonal work only

23. What are your biggest problems **now**?

Getting money for business	= 33%	Not enough sales	=	31%
Getting supplies	= 25%	Too many businesses the same as yours	=	16% m
Finding a good place(s) to sell	= 20%	Workers	=	2%
		Your lack of skills	=	4%
Transport	= 8%	Records	=	3%
Fuel	= 2%	Laws/regulations	=	2%
Tools/machines	= 19%	Other	=	4% Inflation / 2% Health Problems (smoky cooking fires) / 2% Robbed / 3% Other

Future

24. If in the future you cannot go home, do you want to:

Expand your business here	= 89%	Expand elsewhere	=	30% m
Get a job here	= 9% m	Get a job elsewhere	=	7% m

25. If in the future the government or another organisation was to offer you help for your business, what is useful?

Finding new customers	=	38%
Finding a new place	=	22%
Training for better skills	=	30%
Training in accounting	=	10%
Change in laws/regulations/taxes	=	6%
Getting a loan	=	57%
Other	=	2% = No Problems / 2% = Supply Difficulties / 3% = Other

Other Details

26. If there are any other details from the questions before, or interesting points (eg, person is disabled or it is the only business like it in the camp, etc), please put details below

Other details have been added to each questions answers. All the categories in Questions 13-15 and 22-25 were correlated against Questions 5-10 and 16-20 – except for the men/women and rural/urban balances, no other correlations were significant.

Thank you

www.ingramcontent.com/pod-product-compliance
Ingram Content Group UK Ltd.
Pitfield, Milton Keynes, MK11 3LW, UK
UKHW050226150426
5217IPUK00023B/1669